# CHARLIE'S A BROAD

# CHARLIE'S A BROAD

Travails in Fern Parts

by Charlie Farquharson

with photygrafts by Valeda Drain Farquharson

Copyright © Don Harron 1994

All rights reserved. The use of any part of this publication reproduced, transmitted in any form or by any means, electronic, mechanical, recording or otherwise, or stored in a retrieval system, without the prior consent of the publisher is an infringement of the copyright law. In the case of photocopying or other reprographic copying of the material, a licence must be obtained from the Canadian Reprography Collective before proceeding.

Canadian Cataloguing in Publication Data

Harron, Don, date.

Charlie's A Broad!: Travails in Fern Parts

ISBN 0-7715-9064-4

1. Voyages and travel – Humor. 2. Canadian wit and humor (English).* I. Title.

PS8565.A66C5 1994    C818'.54    C94-931505-2
PR9199.3.H37C5 1994

1  2  3  4  5  FP  98  97  96  95  94

Cover and text design by Counterpunch
Cover photo by Valeda Drain Farquharson

Macmillan Canada wishes to thank the Canada Council, the Ontario Ministry of Culture and Communications and the Ontario Arts Council for supporting its publishing program.

Macmillan Canada
A Division of Canada Publishing Corporation
Toronto, Ontario, Canada

Printed in Canada

This book is dedicated
to the dedication of our travel agent
Sandra McMillan

# Pree-am Bull

It wuz yer Blotto Sex-fur-Nine that dun it. Valeda, the wife and farmer sweetart has bin playin them numbers games since time in memoriam. Not me. I figger tryna be a farmer nowadaze is enuff of a gambol without payin' fer the privy-ledge of loosin' yer shirt. So I never tuck a weakly chants with my spared change. But the wife's bin dippin' into her egg munny regler as crockwork.

This pass Chrismuss she put wun of them blottery tickits in my hung-up stockin' alongside a ornj and a bit a cole. It wuz the oney gift she cud think of fer the man hoo has everything but munny.

Call it bug-inners luck, but this heer vergin' clicked on his first go-round. Wen them balls hit on ther bottoms on the Blotto Teevy show Noo Yeerseve the wife pert neer had apple-pleck-sey. Them liddle sfeers cum up with all my nummers but one.

Valeda sez if Ida got all the nummers I'd a bin a malted millyumair, but as it turn out I wuz still mebby a quarter a millyumair.

Right away I got thinkin about wat I cood do with all that munny. I'm not yer greedyguts. I figgerd I had enuff fer to run a furstrate farm. That's wen I found out havin' munny kin be more cumplycated than not havin' it. The wife sed, sure, run that munny rite into the ground. Terned out wat she wanted morn ennything wuz fer to git offa the old homested, and live in town hard by yer shop-in malls in one of them condom min-imums. Maid us start thinkin ther were a lotta ways to spend a lotta munny. I reelized it'd make the woeman mizzerbull fer life if I tuck all this prize lute and ploud it rite back onto my land to noah vale.

Wen the noose of our win got into the papers we found out everybuddy else had ideers about how to spend our well-gotten ganes. We was beseeched by vackyume cleener sails-men and sockbrokers and mewchill funders. Worsen that, we herd frum famly members hoo haddent giv us the time a day in dunkys yeers, third cussins once or twice remooved (and fer good, we thot . . . ).

We deecided if this wuz gonna be our lifestiles bein' ritch and fame-us then we better ignore sitch Leaches with our undivide attenshun. So Valeda and I sat down by arselfs and had a titta-tit. Stayin' on the farm or even moovin into town wood bring us rite smack up agin the harsemint of all the peeple hoo wuz buggin' us and beggin us fer a peece of our ackshuns. I wuzn't reddy fer to jist throw in the trowel an' go to town with Valeda, but I'm heddin' fer three scores and ten, no time to start brakin' new ground on my own land. Nosirree bob, it were time fer a cumprymize twixt the wife and me, so we deesided to do neether yer one.

We hadda drive all the waze to Soo Sweet Marie fer to pick up the check. That give us time fer to think over our opshins. The wife sed if she coodn't moove into town she wanted to go south fer the winter, and she didn't mean jist a few miles south, like down to Coldwater where we have relations. So ware to go furst? Well, the winter were cold enuff to freeze the nots offa bloo sprooce, so the wife sed she wanted to lay somewares on one of them sunsy beeches. After farty yeers of marge she wanted to go all the way in sum place with a topical climax. She wuz thinkin' Florider, but I herd that the blaim place wuz chalk fulla Canajuns, and wat's the good of goin' to furn parts if yiz don't cum up agin furners?

So I got out the old Joggafree and started lookin' up spots in yer Carbeen. There's not as many i-lands down in yer West Undys as we got in yer Gorgin Bay (thirtythousand accorn to yer sadisticks) but them Carbeen peeples got a lot bigger ones. Lookin at that map, we figgerd if weer hedded into the big bloo yunder, we wanted a dustynation biggern a flyspeck. Besides yer Grenader, yer Virgins, yer Turks and Caucuses, and yer Lessor Ant Tillys, they got big suckers like Jaymaker, Trinitydad, Barbydose, Hatey, Poortoe Reekyo, and yer Dumminny-kickacan Republicans, ware them Bloojays mostly cums frum. Not to menshun the biggest lanmass of them all, witch is yer Cuber. And that's ware I deecided to hed fur. Valeda, she had red summers in a maggazeen, (she thinks it wuz yer Shat Elaine), that them Cubists had sumthin' goin' fer tooryists that nobuddy elts cud offer . . . two magickle words . . . NO TIPPING!

## Yer Past Port to Delite

T he mottoe of yer Farquharson clan is "Fidel Itty and Farty Tewd" so it seamed right that we had chose the home of the Cubist dicky-tater fer our maid-in start to see a third of yer wurld. But it terns out that ther's more ta gittin' outa Canda than ther is ta gittin' outa Parry Sound. Seams that wunce yuh put yer mined to goin sumwares intresting yuh hafta apply yerself fer what they call a past-port.

To do the ackshul applyin' I figger I'd take the wife along nex time I go to Hawgtown fer to drop off a Tamworth and a Poland Chiner porker at the Canned A-packers. So I went down with the old haff tun secund hand pickup. (That's the truck not the wife. I'm not one of yer Showviznist mail prigs. Yer showiznist is sumbuddy hoo thinks HARASS is two seprit words.)

After I drop off our porkers, I drug Valeda over to this place hard by yer Teetin Senter called the Antrium ware the Departmint of Exterminal Affares has set up a pastport shop fer to git yiz outa the country. And . . . let's not fergit this . . . back in agin!

The pastport offiss wuz up on yer twelf story, so we noo

Help! Wanted.

we weer deeling with a hire-up buncha sibble serpents. First thing we hadda do is take a nummer jist like in the summer wen you wants a Basking Robin nice creem koan. We got a hy one so this give us plenny of time to go out on Yung Street and git our pitchers took.

Valeda kinda shrivel wen she seen her past-port pitcher, and wuz resolvent never to look like a ax murdress agin. Meentimes we hadda go back up yer 12 flores and fill out both our forms wile we et our take-away lunch frum the Burgler King.

Valeda thot they wuz kinda nozey askin about things like the dait of yer berth, yer martial stattus, and the culler of yer hare at present. Wen it cum to listin our children under the age of sixteen, we put NUN TO SPEEK OF, on accounta Orville's a umpteen-ager. Wen they ast fer our boy's permamint address Valeda put . . . AT HIS GURLFREND'S HOUSE. I didnt know what to put down fer SEX. Valeda suggested INFREEKWENT. She reely bristled wen the yung girl beehind the counter ast me if that wuz one word or two.

# Yer Grate Excape

To git us to Cuber, Valeda foned up the Voyeur Buss-peeple. They seamed vurry plezzant; asked her "How are yiz today?" and the wife give her standerd ree-ply: "Fare to Middlin!" The Voyeur girl sed back quick as yer wink: "That'll be $18.75 one way." The wife told her we didden wanta go to Middlin or even Penustangextinguishmachine, and besides Valeda insist on a round triptickit. The buss girl sed "To ware?" Valeda shouted: "To rite back HERE, ninny!!!"

But the wife didden reelize that this topical Eyeland of Cuber is compleatly detached frum Norse Amerca by 90 miles of saltywater. This wuz a shock to Valeda's sistern. Now the wife don't mind passing time with yer water; we had a ring tail snorter of a crooze on yer Saggymoe outa Graven-hearse last summer wen we had a cuppla daze-off between us gittin' in the hay and gangthrashing with our nabers. She jist wunderd why we cooden hed fer Florder furst, and then take a Cubist boat acrost. Wat she din't reelize that water travvle tween Cuber and the Staits is a matter of pollticks. The States has put a unbargo on Fiddle Castroil's Socialite State, and so all the water travvle so far is only goin' the wun way, frum Cuber to My-Ammy, compleatly unoffishully and in pritty small boats. This meens if Canajuns wanna git to them Cubists we gotta take wings and fly. Now that's ware the wife and former sweetart gits down-rite parry-annoyed. She don't bleeve the good Lard intend us to go hire'n the haymow. Valeda has only flewd the once and that wuz back in the lait thurtys. (Not Valeda's late thurtys, but before World War eleven when she wuz a liddle slip of a teenyaged thing.) She hadda go to a funeereal of a ded ant in Wayburned Sassakatchewin, and sumbuddy tocked her into gittin on a plain. Them wuz the days wen Air Candida wuz called yer Teazy-A and I bleeve they still had the outside toilits.

Well sir, no sooner had Valeda tuck off in that old plain, than she started to git a pane in herear. (Hold yer presses, Ed., that's spaced-out rong. It's her ear, not rear.) In them daze nobuddy wuz yet jet setters, the injuns wuz all props up in the air, and everybuddy wuz under sum pressyer when they got up abuv yer clowds. But in them pree-wore times ther wuz a Register Nurse on bored to help yiz out. Nowadaze they calls them stewyasses, witch is the hy-tex word fer fly-in waitruss, and if yuh feels a bit sickey they can't give you much morn a cuppla Assburn or a void-bag. But back in them pre-wore daze, them Registerd flyin' Nursys wuz supposed to give propper hospiddle care. So Valeda wrung the bell fer the Stewyass to cum, and tole her she needed sumthing fer to stop the pane in her eers. All this Reegisturd Nirse give her wuz a liddle box with a pare of Chicklit in it! That stuff never did nuthin' fer her eery pane atall, and it took about three weeks of Valeda stompin' with her boots and shakin' her hed at the saim time fer to git them dam Chicklits outa her ears.

It's not the takin' off Valeda minded so much as the headin' in fer a landin' that give her the Willies. I tole her mebby we cood parry-shoot her in like they do with eleckshun candied-dates, but she seen that Mary Pop-ins moovy and she cooden figger out how that Dooly Androoze kep her skirt down. Valeda didden want a buncha them forners lookin up her dress and she figgerd hers'd be rap around her eers.

It wuz anuther cold snapper that tern the tide. Jist wen Valeda wuz gittin' into a flap about flyin', Arthur mommeter hit the brass munky ware it herts, forty fore blow! That dun the trick. She flip-flapped and we wuz off.

# Yer Wiled Blew Yonder

Never mind gittin all the way to Fiddle Castroiland, it tuck us quite a time to git to the Malted airport in Trauma, now called after one of our preevious encumbrances, Leslie Piercin'. And it wernt no ormery airport. It hadda interminabull number of interminals. Furst off, we wuz confuse between the naims Air Canda and Canajun Air. We thot that one wuz the saim as the uther oney in French sints it wuz writ backerds. So we got confuse about wether we shood be at yer Interminable Number Two, or Number Three?

Valeda seen a sine witch sed sumthin like "PARK YER FLY" so we druv in and ast direckshuns. They tole us that we shood be-hedded fer Interminable Number Three (witch is called yer Trillyum on accounta all the munny it cost to bild it). Them Parkin Flires also sed we cud park our truck with them and take a bus. Valeda give me one of them "I told ya so" looks, but this bus wernt Cuber-bound. It only took us frum our parkin lot to the interminable building. That ride wuz the quickest part of our hole trip. In no time atall we wuz standin' in line with our luggridge fer wat seam ours and ours. I think the hole country wuz evaccinatin' therselfs south that day. And I thot I'd git a hurnya frum carryin on with all our sootcases, but finely we got to exchange mosta our overwate bags fer liddle peeces of paper. This aloud us to git bored on wat a loudspeekin' voice called yer BOING Seven Eleven, witch tern out to be one of them Dumbo Jets. But we were still pritty loded with our carrying on wat they call ham baggidge, all that stuff yood hate to see end up in Ma-Dred or Barf-a-loner or sumwares elts, and havin' a better time than you.

But first we hadda pass a masheen that tested our mettle. I pass musterd okay after I decoined myself a cuppla times, but Valeda kep cumming back and making that funny noise on the masheen that sed she wuz still full of klinkin. Them serchers looked at the wife as if she wuz a regler terrier-ass! She cooden seem to perduce wat wuz cozzing the trubble and no wunder. It were the steal ribs in her mother's old coarsit, and ther's no way she wuz gonna let herself out of that. I thot they mite try to put her bawdy thru the saim rubber curtins as checked out our baggidge, but they finely took Valeda inside ther offiss to anuther X-Rated masheen that yuh cood stand up to and be seen thru. They seen that she wernt loded with booey nives or baynits or anythin elts leethal, but they tole her that if she had tried to git into Cuber that way they mite have had to cut her stays short.

I thot we mite git on the plain next, but I reckund without

yer Judyfree. This wuz a cut-rait shop ware yuh cood git goods on sail without no guvmint sintax intyfeerence of any kind. Oney trubble is the wife and I are nunsmokers and tee-total-tit-aryans, so the wife loded up on tilet water and poorfumes. I jist bot a fantsy ballsy-point founting pen fer to start jottin down wat it's like to be a broad.

By the time we got to our gait, everybuddy wuz sitting around reddy to bored the plain. We wuz called up by nummers Bibel stile. ("The last shall be first and the furst shall be last.") We cum first cuz we brung up yer reer of the plain. We went back pritty neer as far as the Pope's noze.

Valeda didden show her nerfs too much until they tole us all the Safe-tea feechers of yer aircrap, like ware all them Urgency Exits wuz in case we crash. Valeda neer threw up her Gravel pill at that, and I give her one of them barfbags jist in case of pewk. Then they tot us how to look under yer seet to preepair fer bitching over water. Valeda thot the gurl on the pubic undress sistern sed ditching, but wen yuh got yer hole of yer otion blow yuh cant call that a ditch, and beesides, if the wife and I hadda bale arselfs out of a plain after spendin all that munny, yood better prepair to heer sum reel bitching, lemme tell yuh.

Terns out you cant do nuthin with mosta them crashtoys they tells ya about till yuh gits outside the plain, wen you pull a red tag to blow yer vest up, and if that don't work you has to reesort to oral stimmle-ation to puff yerself up. I lernt more about inflation in 2 minits than I ever did watchin the bizness news. They wisht us a plessant jurny and hoped we never brung along no mikey-wave ovins or cellulite fones utherwise we'd all end up floundering in the drink of yer Golf Streem. By this time Valeda look like she wuz havin' locomotive auto-taxi-yuh and wuz too ridge-id to speek.

After all that lechering they give us a blankit and a pilla (in case we had to be up in the air overnite I spose) and then threw us a bag a peenuts like we wuz munkys in a zoo. Neether of us had the nuts cuz it's too hard to git open the packidge unless yuh got yer own teeth. I cant tell yuh too much about the trip after our take-off (witch sounded like a regler hooravacane accorn to Valeda) cuz I wuz on the pill that the wife gimme and fell rite into the arms of Murphyuss. I figger there's no sents in bean awake with no wun to tock to. The wife had a dubble dose of them sleepy pills, but she staid awake the hole time. She sed at one point the pile-it tole us we wuz over Jorgia, but Valeda looked down and didn't see nairy a peech. In fack, no seenery almost all the way.

Valeda wuz so blaim edgy by the time they surfed us fud, that she et my meel asswell as hers. I wuz still out like yer porsh lite. She sed the best thing she et was a peece a cheece but tryna git it out of the packedge she darn neer give herself a hermia. She sed it wuz a good thing she wuz arm with a stake nife. After all that fuss about conjeeled weppins at yer areport and then they hand eech of us a cuppla sharp nives on our own.

Watever the fud wuz like, I mist it. In fack, I didden wake up till after the plain landid. Valeda wuz landin' it all by herself with her heels dug into the flore wen I woke up jist afore them liddle bumps wen we hit the ground. I tole the wife to keep practising her land-ins till she wuz smooth. But all the uther passinjers applodded her.

We debarked in th' oppsit order frum gittin' on. So the Farquharsons wuz last to git out and git off. Ded last, smatter of fact, cuz I coodn't git outa my seet. I have never felt so peckuleyer sints the hay-waggin fell on me back in '48. I cooden moove. I felt as if I had sum kind of stroke, mebby a case of antjemima pectoralis (witch is hy-tex talk fer hartattack.) But it wernt troo. Valeda reeleesed me frum my parry-alysis by undoin the buckel of my safe-tea belt.

FLORIDER    GRAND BANANAS

# Cuber

HATEY

HAV
ANNA

VERY
DAIRYO
BEECH

JAW
MAKER

GWAN
TAMMY
MOE

# Castro Rated

By the time we got outen yer aircrapft, everybuddy elts wuz outa site, and the oney person we seen at the bottom of the airstares wuz a Cubist in army fateegs with camelflatch all over it. Wen he seen Valeda and me his eyes pop open like that TeeVee popcorn in a bag. He started talkin in sum kinda forn langridge and waivin' his arms but it wuz all a mistry to us. The general idee frum his jestyers wuz that we wuz to folly him. So we dun it, cuz he had on a unyform, and we didden no ware elts to go.

He never took us to enny bilding ware we figgerd the rest of them voyeurs went. Insted he tuck us to the uther end of yer runaway ware wuz parked a army veehickle looked like a Wirld Wore Too Brengun carryer. He give the sine fer us to hop inn, and before yuh cood say Jacky Robinsun we wuz outa yer areport and on the rode to Habanner. (I allways thot it wuz Havanner, but them Cubists don't seem to mind their B's and V's like we do our Pees and Cues.)

Our driver fella didn't say nuthin to us on the jurny, jist kep smilin like he wuz offal glad to see us. He staired at me a lot as if he alreddy noo me. Jist as well he didden speek, cuz us Farquharsons never lerned the Cubist lingo. Valeda claims they speak like Spanish or mebby Porchgeese instedda havin ther own kinda tock. She still has all the lawn-playing reckerds of that Mumble King, Ex-Saviour Coogat, and she rememberd how that fella Rickety Rickardo tocked wile playin' his Congo drum and singin "Baby Lou" on the TV show *I Luv Loosly*.

It were dark wen we got into yer Cubist's capitol, and ther wernt menny street lites on the side, jist on yer mane drags. The driver tuck us in fronta a big pubic square with statutes all over it, and they wuz all pritty well lit. We wuz excorted into a big bildin that looked offal familyer. Fer a minit yoo

wood have thot we wuz in the States cuz this place look jist
like yer Capitolist Dome in Warshinton on yer D.C. But this
musta bin a carbine copy. We climed and climed stares.
Suddinly we wuz ushied into a room fulla beerds in unyform.
Our young driver wuz sorta cleen shave like me and
Valeda, but these suckers look like our Canajun Fathers of
Conflagellation with face-fuzz hangin down frum their chintz
several Cuban inches.

This hairy grupe was all dress in cammyfladge fiteegs too,
and they seem even gladder to see us than our yung bear-faced
driver. They wissled fer sum yung gurl to bring in a waggin with
a Roosian teepot (they call it a sammyvar), not to menshun a
boddle of ther lokel screech. I wuz waitin fer them to give us a
sine to dig in to all this. No wurds spoke, but lotsa jestyers like
we wuz playin' Shrades at a party. Valeda and me dun our best
to keep our ends up of this dum non-conversation. Valeda wuz
about to ast if it wuz a song titel and with how menny sillabulls,
but afore we cood git enny anser, (and our hands on a cuppa
tee!), a new fella cum into the room with a must-ash, a bizness
soot but no beerd. He started talkin' to us but he didden sound
like yer Cubist, and certny not yer Anglican Saxon.

Wile we stud there parched, the fella stud in frunta the tee
waggin, and tocked at us fer a long time, and seam to expeck
a reeply wen he wuz finnished. We jist plaid dumm, witch wuz
certinly the way we wuz feeling ennyways. So this fella started
with the jestyers too. He pick up a lump of shugger and brung
out wat look like a order book fer us to sine. He seam to be
asking us how much shooger we wood take. By gol, I figgerd
we wuz finely gittin to the refrashmints. I sed, "Two lumps."

Fer the first time sumbuddy talked in Anglican-Saxon. "You
are In Glaze?"

I sed, "No I'm in farming."

"You are from Moscow???"

Valeda sed, "No.We're frum Parry Sound." Everybuddy
scratch their heds at the same time.

"Parry Sound, Ontario, Canada."

Everybuddy picked up on that last word. They started rumblin amungst theirselfs as we herd, "Two wrista. Hoe tell. Pronto."

Terns out they thot Valeda and me wuz a Serviet Aggravaculcher Dalligation. They hadden had one of them in a dunky's age, witch is why they wuz so glad to see us. But they hoped we'd take home a million bags a shooger, not jist two lumps. We never did git our tee.

Deer Boy:

Well we finely got heer but not after sum avenchers. Yer father slep thru the plain trip. I never. We got lait at our hotel but we manedge to git in sum supper. Don't let them heffers pick at the silo too much.

Yer luv-in muther.

## "One-Ton-a-Merde, eh?"

That yung Koo-bah jeapdriver tuck us rite back to the airport, pick up our baggridge without no cusstoms, and maid sure we got to our hoetell. We found out lader that sints the Roosians don't have enuff cowpecks fer to buy their shooger, Cubists figger Tooryism has gotta be their Nummer One hevvy industree. (I figger the saim thing fer Canda if we kin deetract enuff Yanks to cum back despike us taken away their World Serious.)

Ther wuznt enny Yanks there, unless you count them Ewe Ass Murines down to Gwam-tannymoe Bay. Them uninvited aileens bin there since 1934 on a 99 yeer leese. Ya'd think it wuz the Cubists that didden want Yanks in here after that eva- sion they pulled back in '61 with their U.S. grunts at yer Baying of the Pigs. But it wernt them Koobans put the unbargo tween yer States and them, it were Yank forn polissy egged on by all them ex-Cubist Castero-haters in My-Yammy. Canda don't have no such prestrickshuns. We wuz the furst country to start this tooryist boom that's now goin' on down there.

Wen we got to our hoetel's lobby ther wuz a geetar-wrist and a bingo drummer fer to welcum us. (Valeda sez it's bongo not bingo drums, but I figger it cant hurt to have a little vowel movement on yer holidaze.) They wuz playin' that French song "One Ton a Merde, eh?" (I herd it so menny times in the daze after that I figger it wuz yer Cubist Nashnul Antrum.)

We wuz told we cud still git sum fud, cuz peeple wuz still standin in the buff, eh? That jist meens yuh kin grab wat yiz want yerself without bein' serfed. Valeda sez she bin eatin' that way all her life, but it wuz nice to be able to leev the dishes. When we went to git lined up fer our grits, we found that mosta the cafeteria soceity peeple there wuz Canajuns. And the fud wuz Canajun . . . chicking pot pie . . . Terns out later that the cheef Sheff wuz frum Winnypeg!

After our late nite snatch, we wuz took by a belled-buoy to our rooms. He carried all our luggridge and never hung around to be tipt. And it wuz a fur peece he drug them bags too. The hoetell itself wuz jist a little bilding, and all the rooms wuz allover the place in seprit little uther bildins, called villans.

The Cubists have their own speshul secure-a-titty sistern. They put the rong number on yer roomkey, so if ya loose it,

nobuddy elts kin figger out witch room to git in! Unfartunitly
it works jist asswell on the ones hoo blong there.
    Our villan wuz not too noo lookin, but cleen and neet. Wen
we open the frunt door ther wuz a rore like a toronaido. I figgerd it wuz yer poundin of yer serfs on yer beech but it tern
out to be the air condition masheen. Since we cum all the ways
here to git outa the cold we terned it off. Besides, we found
wen we open the winders it wuz a regler steddy breeze (sorta
like bein in Ragina all the time only the tempachure is more
topical).
    That first nite Valeda wuz nun too impress, speshully wen
she started to eggzamin wat she calls yer deck-whore of our
place. The walls wuz all red like that fancy House inhibited by
yer Canajun Sennit. I figger the Guvmints use that culler to keep
them Sentaurs awake. Valeda wurried that she mite not sleep
much heer eether, speshully wen she got into bed and staired
up at the seeling and ther she wuz, stairin back at herself in a
meeror. No refleckshun on them Cubists, but wat in the Sam
Hill is the pint of havin' a look-in glass way up on the rufe?
    Trubble cum the nex morning wen I tride to shave standin
on the bed. I had a dickins of a time tryna git latherd up stum-
blin' round, and wuz gonna try it mebby lyin down, but Valeda
let me use the mirra in the baffroom after she finisht up her
absolutions.
    The mistry of the overhed mirra wuz solv at breckfust wen
a nice granmuther frum Hamilton (Ontaryio, not Barenooda)
tole us we had bin sleapin' in wat useter be a bore-deller.
Valeda had never herd the werd before, so I X-planed to her
that it wuz a place that housed bizzy bodies, and we had ackshully had one in Parry Sound back in yer notty twentys, rite
there in the middla town, not far frum the old Orr house ware
Bobby wuz borne.
    Well, the wife wuz all fer up and takin our leev rite then
and ther, but that Hamilton woman tole her this all had happen decadents ago durin the rane of that old dicky-tater, Bap

Teaster, hoo wuz in coe-hoots with the Mafiascos of yer Cosy
Nostril. But she sed nuthin' like that wuz goin' on with them
Castro Socialites. Their morales wuz jist as Pure-it-tannicle
as Valeda's . . . smatter of fack, this seeniory sittizen of a
granmuther had bin to Habanner back in yer fiftys before
it had bin Castrorated, and she sed that this Bapteesta wood
put down vilent resolutions agin himself by openin' all the sin-
nymaws fer free, and showing fornograftic moovys. That put
the kybo on his Rayjeem bein overthrone. I gess Castro
manedge to overcum him in '59 wen Bapteesta run outa durty
moovys.

We cum here to Cuba fer yer sunsy beeches. And wat a
munster of a beech! Makes Wasaggy hard by Orillya look like
a backyard sanbox. It seam to go fer miles alongside of that
water that looks deep bloo fur out, but close to shore was more
like turkwazz. (Valeda calls it Actra Murine.) I had brung along
my old bloo bathe-in soot that I had swum in before the wore
at Camp Boredom. It has straps round yer sholders like a
brassear but Valeda tole me to creem myself pritty good as this
is a topical climax and I cood still git bernt thru the big hole
up yer O-zone.

Nun of the men on that beech wuz pertectin therselfs as
mutch as me frum sitch ultry violents. They wuz all bear
breasted. The wimmen mite aswella bin, wearing them teeny
weeny bickaneenys that look like their maid of two band-ades
and a plug. Ther wuz 1 Jermin womman wocked by bare as a
bird on top. The wife looked away wen Miss Udders cum by,
or to be more accurit, she looked MY way to see if I wuz lookin
away, witch I wuzn't. Fine upstanding Holsteen spessimin of
a woman.

Valeda kept on a-greesin herself, but I kept fergittin to do
it, so finely she solv the problem by burro-ing me up to my
neck in all that gritty stuff. That way I wooden burn and also
coodn't eezly see if ther wuz any more prominaiding nude-a-
titty.

But after that we both had a tern gittin wetted in yer otion. I brung along wat they call a Pursonal Inflation Deevice, a Canajun Tire's innertoob fer to help me flote, but Valeda sed I wooden need it. She has Martime ruts and has tasted otion water before. My gol, she's salty! (The otion, as well as Valeda.) Taists offal but it sure keeps ya up! Valeda floted as well as I did but without no toob. She sed salty water is boyant. (I spose, in her case, it wood be gallant.) We both felt a liddlc gilty that wc wuz rumpin' in warm water wen all our fella snoebirds back home wuz freezin ther talefethers off. We noo them poor critters wuz probly fridge-id, wile we wuz both in heat.

Valeda puts the sun blox to Charlie

Valeda wuz content to stay on the beech all day puttin the blocks to herself with a bucket a creem and reedin a Harlotquin novel. She wanted us to go lookin' fer them big see-shells that wen yuh holds them up to yer ear it sounds jist like air conditioning. But Cuebans don't seem to have no big conchy shells round their parts. They jist have crabs that skitter along lookin' at yuh sidewaze. I did find a big ded green thing looked like a infint's portable potty but it tern out to be the shell of a coke-nut.

Yestidday, I deranged to git myself on a busstoor. Wen I ast the Cubist Hoetell manger ware the buss wuz goin, he sed it wuz takin tooryists to see his country's Undyground! Valeda's not too politickle so I give her the faretheewell and got on bored.

First thing cot my tension wen we got outside the tooryist aria (witch is marked off as a speshul slubdivision jist like the ritch parts of Canda) wuz that the rest of yer hole of Cuber cood do with a good paint job. That "Culler yer Wirld" bunch wood make a fartune heer, cheerin' up yer clap-bored by slappin' on a few cotes. But not yer Cube cars fer the most parts . . . If Cubists is shorta paint, they must save it to splash it all on their well-use cars. Passin them in our buss it wuz like ridin' past one of them anteek carrallys yuh seeze back home on weakend.

All these Cubist cars is shiny and well-kept considerin' ther all well inta their mid thurtys. They's all Amerken imports frum before fifty-nine on accounta the unbargo, pluss the odd noo car, sum Laddas frum yer Serviets. I ast the bussdriver ware them old moddles got ther spair parts. He sed they wuz all hand-maid at home. Every driver in Cuber has a mechanick of his own . . . hisself.

We past akers of funny looking plants that looked like green porkypines with ther pricks stickin up in the air. They wuz called seezle and they cremate hemp witch is used fer ropes, sept with our younger ginration hoo tries to smoke it. Our farmers back home hopes to grow it, cuz it makes good paper and cardbored and wood save frum our forsts frum distinction, but Ottawar is nervuss about Dope on a Rope. They also make berth-countroll pills out of the stuff . . . don't ask me how . . . and don't ask me why neether, cuz Cuber is still Roaming Cathlick at the saim time as it's Commonest. The Pope still demands that his R.C.'s git by with their rithm secksun. So when it cums to reeperduction that must put them Cubists on the horns of a reel enema.

Yer Cuban Undyground tern out to be a cave. Nothin to do with Castro-haters hoo think he is a Cuban heel. Only plitickle part of it wuz the fack that slaves use to hide in it centurions ago wen they wanted to excape ther croolmasters.

They had a tickit wickit in frunt and stares leeding down

to it. Utherwise I wooden have noan it frum a hole in the ground. But caves is intrusting fer yer simble-minded cuz their cuvverd top to bottom with stoned eyesickles called Stalack Tites (down frum yer top) and Stalag Mites (up frum yer bottom). Sumtimes, after neons of yeers of drippin on eech uther they meet and form a stone piller, but my gol, a good bilder can do the same thing outa seement in a few minits!

Today we went farther afeeld for grazin cuz Valeda wuz gittin fed up with all this Norse Amerkend fud. After five daze of Riced Kristys and scramble aigs she wanted sumthing more eggsawtick. The Winnypeg sheff suggested cheese dogs or that garlicky sassidge Winnypeggers call cowbassos, but the wife wanted sum lokel Cubism kweezeen. (Fore we left Parry Hoot she had maid me a Spainish breckfust called "Wave-Ass Raunch-Eros" which to me jist seemed like chilly fride aigs.) But she wuz gittin downrite frust-rate with all this chicking pop pie fer lunch and Barby-cute ribs fer dinner. So Valeda tole the mangemint of the hoetel to book us with reservayshins at a Cubist restrunt that don't have tooryists in their client-tail. (That's a fantsy word fer cussdummers).
    Valeda brung along a little Berlitz book that tot yiz how to tock the lokel limgo. She tride to teech me usefull frazes like "No hablo Espanola" witch sounded to

wealthy
plowboy on
the beech

me like "I never lived in Espanola." The one she wanted me to remember most of all so's I wooden disgraze arselfs wuz "Don Day Ell Bananyo dee Cab Alairos?" witch meens where's the men's can? (Wen the time cum I fergot it on the way to the biffy, but that waiteruss understood me wen I went back to jestyers and dun my desprit peepee dance.)

The Hoetell sent us to a seefud restrunt that speshulizes in Lam Goost. Now that may sound like a cross-bred Ramduck but it's nuthin' to do with yer animule kinkdom. Lam Goost is Cubist fer lobstir, but ther's one big differents frum yer Martime lobster in the maine. These suckers got no claws, not even subordinit ones. Don't ast me how they deefends themselfs. (They must feel like us Canajuns wen we faces up to Glowball compytishun.) But to make up fer the suckyoulint meet ya mite miss on the claws, the Lamgoost lobstir got the biggest peece of tail I've ever seen.

Valeda thot the best thing about the hole evenin wuz not the fud but the mewsickal a-company-ment. Two fellas with geetars and a girl sung and played with us all nite. And they never sung "One Ton a Merde" even once. Valeda spoke Spainish fer to give them a reequest . . . "Bossa Nova." (I always thot the Bossa Nova wuz that Elberta oil fella, Bob Blare.) The girl played wat sounded like wood spoons, excepting they looked more like liddle tilet seats. Valeda sez they're called Cascarets. This here tree-o give out with a song that even I new: "The Girl frum Yuppy Neema." Valeda sung the words and the learyicks all by herself, a capulco. Not to be outdun by the wife and former sweethart, her hazbin went naytif with a rummy drink called yer Cuba Livery, and it maid me so blaim tipsy I tipped everybuddy on the way out.

Nex time we hedded fer the see-shore, the wether wuz clowded fer a change, and there wuz Red flags stuck in the sands. It wernt a Commonest celibation, it wuz lifegards worning us not to swim cuz the see wuz runnin high with under-toes and a lotta swells on the beech. Valeda didn't mind, she

sez bein' a woeman she unnerstans about the red flag bein' up.
She wuz by this time pritty beeched out too, and after our
restrunt venture into Cubist culcher she was anxshuss to git
back to Habanner by daylite and see how the reel Koo-ban pee-
ons lived.

So we sined up fer a busstoor that inclooded a big niteclub
show, yer Tropickanner Reevyou with a lotta boomps-yer-daizy
dancin' girls. Valeda wernt too sure if that wood innerduce us
to troo Carbean culcher but I tole her it wuz all part of the Toor
packedge . . . churches and guvmint bildins during the day, and
after son-set, niteclub girls mooving their abominable mussles.

On the way we seen more 1950s cars than you kin shake
a joystick at, and a lotta rickety lookin' busses that stopped
fer ornery peeple. A lotta pederastrians hung up their thums
wen we past, but Toorism don't stop fer lokels. In Habanner
they even have speshul Toorismo Police fer to look after us if
we gits to be a stray. I kinda wisht they'd bin rite there wen
we got offa the bus, cuz we wuz surrounded by childern all
yelling "Cheeklit! Cheeklit!" Terns out that chompin gum is
the meejum of X-change among yer yunger Kooban ginration.
They're may be no tip-in on that i-land, but them liddle beg-
gers sure maid up fer it. But they wuzn't after our munny, jist
our gums.

We finely took refuse in a church, where we found a plack
on the floor tellin us this wuz the berryin spot of yer Sheer duh
Deeperbill, the famousexplorer and mitey worrier hoo had
drum up all that furry trade round Hudson's Bay in yer sixteenth senchury. But he end up here in Koo-bah insted of on a
ice-flow in our friggid waters. I gess in such a topical climax it
wernt hard fer him not to think of the Bay.

Habanner is reely divide into two parts, yer noo and yer
old. The old part is fulla Cathlick churches and the noo part is
fulla guvmint bildins. Best part about yer old town I thot wuz
a bar freakwent by that ded Yank writer Ernst Hemaway. I
never herd of him but Valeda nose all about the importance of

being Ernst. She even red a book he writ called "Yer Son Also Rise." I cood have writ the same book about our Orville gittin' up a cuppla hours lader than us every mornin, but Valeda sez Hemaway's book is mostly about Tory Adores, them bull-fitters in the Mickey Mouse hats.

Heer in Koo-bah he dun a book called "Yer Old Man in the See," all about a old fishyman hoo never catches nuthin'. Sounded to me like contempuary Noofunland . . . this book, Valeda sez, won him a Nobel prize, but he got nuthin', not even Honnerbull Menshun, frum Parrysound or Macteer.

The last of the Moeheatos

Best thing Urny Hemaway left us wuz a drink he used to sloose down pritty regler called a Moeheato. It's slime jooce, wite rum and fizzy wotter with a sprigga minty leevs stuck in it. They took us to the bar ware he drunk them, and even Valeda had one of them Moeheaters (in onner of litterchur of corse) and she jist giggle like a ninny the resta the trip. So much fer the temprunts vows of the first vice of our Parry Sound W.C. Tee You!

The Guvmint bildins in the noo Habanner ain't used much fer guvmint. They're mostly terned into Exhibitionists fer Torsts. Fr'instants, their own Cubist Common House, yer Nashnul Captall Bildin, is a Mewseeum. Don't seem to be much room fer the voices of yer peeple in this 1 party state. The Precedential Paliss that Dickytaters used to use is now the Museleum of yer Revolution. But this Revlution is oney thirty-five yeers old so wat's the spearit of freedum doin' in a Mewsoleum?

The yot (spelt yachit) that brot Fiddle here fer the start of his evasion is on vue in a huge glass case in the middle of a square. The yot is called Granma, and that's the name of the Habanner newspaper. Valeda wuz impress that they have a hole dayly paper fer femail seenery sittizens.

The biggest square in Havanner is Hosey Marty. He wuz a grate loudspeeker a hunderd yeer ago hoo became shot fur bein agin them Spainish. In frunt of his statute is where Fiddle speeks to his

peeple fer four, five ours at a stretch. No seets nowares. Everybuddy stands it fer that long, incloodin' Fiddle hisself. Koobans are used to standin around, thanks to the shortedge of pubic transport. My most vivy-id mammery of Habanner is them hunderds of peeple standin' in wate fer a buss. We seen them on the way to our nite club, and I sware we seen sum of the saim ones still standin' there on the way back.

That nite club, Yer Tropical Anna, wuz outside in the bare air in the middle of a forist! I gess if it ranes the hole game is called on accounta bein at the merzy of yer ella mints, but this nite she wuz dry as yer boan. I noo the show wuz startin' wen I seen this priddy girl standin next to a tree not fore feet away, in pantys and brass ear and a big bole of froot on her hed. Put me in mind of that old Soused Amerken moovy actoress, Carmen Veranda.

Clothing Shortedge in Cuber

Then the band struck itself up and duzzens of froot-boled chlorines cum frum everywares in them woods fer to fill up the big platform and all the stares leedin to it. Ther may be no new cars or paint or gum in Koobah but ther's no short-edge of cloth mateerial fer fantsy costyumes. Them heddresses they wares must way forty pounds alone. At one point all them chlorines had on shamdeleers witch lit up like the Ontaria Hydra as they kick up ther heals. (Them gurls, not yer Hydra. Them burrocraps jist kick up our raits.) Mine you, not one bear brest in the hole show, like I herd about at yer Lost Vague-ass. I check carefully and thot I seen one girl topfulless. But it tern out to be a false alarum. She wuz waring a minny fleshy-cullerd brassear, and I haddda borry sum binocklers to make sure.

I havent seen sitch brite cullers floatin a round sints last yeer's Sandy Claws prade. It were a feest fer the eyes but a sound fer sore eers. That band wuz louder than the close they wore. The hole nite seem to be a sorta Olimprick contest tween yer singers and yer orkestry as to hoom cood drown the tother. The danzers change costyumes every three or four minit, but the dessybells of noise never let up. I thot every one of them dances seamed to be the same, but Valeda says I betrade my

iggerunce. First off wuz yer congo line, then yer rhumble, follied by yer Saltsy, yer Sambo, yer Mumble, yer Tanglo, yer
Chat-chat-chat, yer Limp Adder, and yer Regg eh? The oney
danztep I cood extinguish frum all the udders wuz yer Limp
Batter, cuz the dancers seem to go limp after they finnished
battern eech uther. Valeda seem almost eggcited by all this. I
dunno wether it wuz the noise or the dressmaking. The noise
never let up. I peefurred the quiet bits wen the audients
applodded. After that nite I figgered yer Koo-bah nashnul antrum wuz
reely "Bessie Mae Moocher." The music went even further
back than their cars. Valeda reckanize a cuppla uthers frum yer
Hits Prade back in the 40's like "A More" and "Perfiddlya." A
loud woman cum out and sang "Bessie Mae" overn over and
then took a role-call of yer Untidy Nations to find out hoo wuz
here. Ther wuz lots frum Spane, Jermny and Ittly, but the
biggest rore cum frum Canda. Seems like us Farquharsons
wuzn't the oney ones on the run frum yer Troo North Strong
and Freeze.

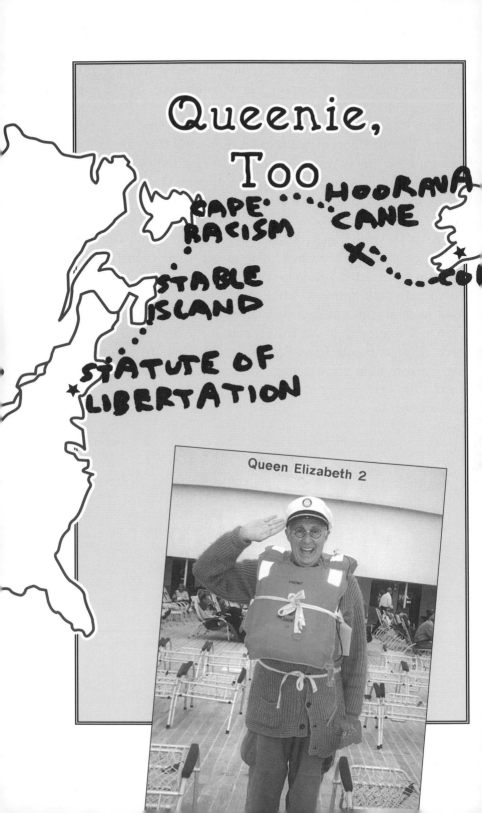

# Queenie, Too

CAPE RACISM

HOORANA CANE

X

STABLE ISLAND

STATUTE OF LIBERTATION

Queen Elizabeth 2

# Home Aloan

We played tooriest fer long enuff to git homesick, but by swinjer, unce we wuz back in friggid Canda we missed them Cubist sunsy beeches. And flyin' wuz still a trile fer the wife and farmer swee-tart. I made sure the wife wuz pritty sedate the hole trip home.

With nobuddy to tock to on the way home aloan, I alluva sudden got homesick fer a place I'd never bin . . . Ire-land. Fer this is ware my four fathers cum frum wen ther taters give out a hunnert and fifty yeer ago. Sints I still had mosta my Blotto Sex-Afore-Nine munny I got the urge to keep on travlin and visit the Old Sods themselves. I figgerd Valeda mite be kinda curio too, fer she's a Drain on her father's side and a Boyle on her muther's, and she mite wanta dig up sum of her incesters.

Viva le Cuba libre!

So help me, if ther'd bin a Airlingus flite to Dubblin or Shammon I think I wooda took it strait frum Cuber. But that Castrode place don't purrmitt no sitch thing as Cubalingus.

Wunce we got close to home Valeda moned that she'd never go travlin' agin. Wen we got inside our own dore, we found we wuz home aloan, but ther wer sines that Orville had bin shackin up with his gurl-frend and it look like he hadden dun a thing round our parts (eggsept her). Hadden even emty the male box, witch wuz pritty full to bustin', lemmy tell yuh.

I check the stock but they wuz in gud shapes (thanx to our luv-in nex dore nabers, Gawd bless'em).

Ther wuz more letters frum sum of them thurty-secund cussins we hadden herd frum in yeers, but at the bottom of our piles ther wuz also a Tooristick advertizemint fer sum Grantoors with gides wood take yiz thru all the chirches and cassles of Yerp without no need to speek the forners' langridge. I wuz timpted to show this to Valeda but her face all lit up as she grab sumthin' elts offa the table.

It wuz a full-culler brasheer that contain a pursnal invite to go croozin with H.M. Queen Lizabath the Secund. Valeda's hands shook as she open it, but it wernt to yer Garding party at the Bucking Ham's Paliss. It wuz frum yer uther Q.E. 2, the otion liner hoo wunce run aground offa Sinjon's New Brunsick and hadda have her bottom scraped after it took five tugs to git her inta her slip.

Valeda put that brushoor down and side to herself, still a mite airysick, but I pick it up and found that we cud git acrost to Grade Brittin by waters, with five days on yer Queen's decks instedda seven ours coop up in a plain. That's how our four-fathers cum here in the first place, with no trace of jetslag.

Not oney that, but we cud land dreck in Ire-land on yer Cork, ware her Boyle peeple cum frum. Valeda sed she'd be reddy to go if we cood git to that peer in NooYork ware the Queen sits fore she takes off, without us gittin' all up in the air agin.

I look it up and sure enuff, we cud git ther on yer Yank Hamtracks rale-rode at the Onion station in Trauma. Jist git into our births, and we wood derive the nex morning in time fer sum quick cross-boarder shoppin' amung yer Blooming Dales and that Navel store, yer S.S. Kressgy, and then hitch on to the big bote that afternoon.

The thot of keepin' her feet parrlell to ground levvil as she went thru forn parts, without havin to be flighty, that wuz wut wun the wife over. (As aginst the thot of stain home and bein badgered by long-lost relatiffs.) So sints it wuz still too cold to plow, harra, or go to seed, we sined up fer wun of them busstoors that'd take us past Ire-land all over the continence of Yerp. I maid all the derangements on the fone with Algon-kyouwin Travells, and the nex week we wuz off, as my gran-father used to say, in a cloud of horshat and small stones.

# Manhatin' I-land

Wen we got offa yer Hamtracks at yer Gramsentral Station, we wuz tole that we wuz mebby niner ten blocks frum the big bote we wuz to sale on that day. Valeda thot it'd mebby be a nice strole, and we cud take in the sites like yer Umpire Estaits Bildin, yer Timed Squares, not to men-shin that crotch-boarder shoppin.

I figgerd we shood let a tacksea take us across the Man-hatin' Island to ware yer Queenie the Tooth got herself docked, unlode our axcess baggidge and then mebby hed fer them departly-mental stores with times to spair. No chants, as it terned out. Yuh woodna bleeved it, but it tuck us as long to git them niner ten blocks acrost Nooyork as it dun to git frum the busstop in Metrapopolitan Parry Sound to the Onion Station in Trauma.

And wat a horny place! Them cars all got one and the driv-vers all uses it even tho' it don't do nun of them no gud. Everybuddy leens on ther own in anser to everybuddy eltses. This Avenoo we wuz tryna cross was well-naimed: Mad-Is-On. Them sidestreets is even wurst cuz they're offal narra fer sitch a big city. Maid Main street in Parry Sound seem like Whinnypeg's Porridge Avnoo. Our taxy wuz a hare's bredth frum the cars eether side of it. Valeda wuz holdin' her noze thinkin about all that carping men-ox-hide cumming outa all them bumper to bumpercars.

Ide allwaze bin tole that life in Nooyork is sposed to be pritty dern swift but lemme tell yuh their mornin rush hour maid a funerall in Flesherton seem like yer Indian-anal-apples speedway . . . If yiz ast me, ther's oney one slution to this sitty's trafficle problim. Tern all the lites to red, and let everybuddy git out and walk. Oney veehickles I seen workin up any speed wuz sum dairdevilled bike riders zoomin in and out tween trucks, and the leeder of the troops on foot wuz a lady joggler in swettypants draggin beehind her a liddle Yorky terror with his eyes bug out. Yer pederastrians all got plugs in ther eers with wires attatch, and I betcha ther all tooned into sum rotten roll stayshin by the way they're jigglin while they're jogglin.

So there we wuz, nowares neer our navel dusty-nation and that meeter is ticky tickin all the time. I seen sines everywares 24 HOUR PARKING, and 1 HOUR PARKING, $6.77; 2 HOUR SPECIAL $9.73 and the gasmeeter in the taxy we wuz parked in sez $10.40! Valeda thot it wuz the time a day, but it were yer taxi-tab, and I seen my Blotto Sex-Afore-Nine munny goin' up in bloo smoke wile we sat ther immoably-ized. I ast the driver wat wuz the coz of all this mess, and he sed "Precedent Clitton!" I sed we allso blaim our pollytishuns fer everything in our country. But he sed it reely wuz Billy Clitton's falt on accounta he wuz in Nooyork that day fer to speek to yer Genruss Dissembly of yer Untidy Notions.

We finely arriv at the sharp end of yer Queenie Too morn a cuppla hours after we tuck that taxy. The driver he wuz happy all the time, jest a wisslin and singin away, untill I tride to pay him in Canajan munny. Wen he seen the Quean's pitcher all in purple, he tern the saim culler. I thot he wuz gonna have a cornery. Valeda finely pade him off with one of her Merkin Espresso travlin checks, and he musta got a wopper of a tip outa the wife and former sweetart, cuz as he druv off he started back wisslin rite away. So that wuz our cross boarder shoppin tour of Nooyork. No shoppin, the wife cross, and me board.

# Yer Queenie Too

She's a big sucker, yer Queen, looks kinda top hevvy and well stacked even if she only has the one in the middel. Makes our Muskokey lake liner yer Seegwin look like a liddle robot. (I don't meen them liddle tin men with chips fer branes, I meen a punt with a cuppla ores on the side.) We wuz justin time to meat the ship accorn to our skedool, but we never got to step insider fer the nex two hours. Tryna git on bored Her Majestic wuz a case of hurryup and wate, jist like wen I wuz in yer Roil Muskoky Dismounted Foot at Camp Boredom.

Ther wuz a Birdish offiser with curlycue must-ashes kep us all in line. I kep wundrin how he kep them spiky mustashes in line, and he tole me he dun it with speshul wacks. He wuz plite but firm in keepin us offa the ship, and we felt we wuz back under Briddish rool, after the udder Kayoss of Nooyork.

They hardly look at our passorts with our offal pitchers durin' the customerry immygration. They wuz more consern with the imprince of everybuddy's creditable cards. They even giv yiz a speshul wun they maid up fer to be used ship-bored. I wunderd how passinjers cood shop in the middel of the otion. Liddle did I noe.

When we wuz aloud on bord we found all our luggridge wadin' fer us outside our stately room. It's also call a cabbin, but a lot smaller than them tooryist ones hard by Parrysound. This cabbin wuz like a tiney moetell room sept ther wuz oney wun little round winder, witch didden open. It wuz called a pore-hole, I spose cuz the water wood pore in if yiz opend up the hole.

Wen the wissle bloo fer take-off Valeeda sed we hadda git up on deck fer to git a glimps of yer Statute of Libertations, the big ole lady with a flashlite in her hand sayin' good ridduns to yer tired, yer poor and yer hevvy laid as we wented our way to Yerp.

We clum up the stares along with all the uther seenery sittizens usin' all hands on the railins to git on deck. We clum and we clum and we clum! I never specked that it wood be so far to git outside. No wunder they call it the poop deck. But this big bote oney has a cuppla outside decks and ther both way uptop. In fack, before yuh kin find yerself outside in yer open air, yuh has to go thru all them expansiv shops that's out to sell off ther doodyfree goods on us tooryists.

Leenin over yer rale we cud see that Big Lady on Bedclose I-land, holdin' the torch fer sumbuddy er uther, and lookin like a crotch between Ann Murry and Marg Snatcher.

The call cum frum sum loudspeeker fer to have lifebote drill. We wuz standin rite beside wun of them big robots, so I figgerd we shood stay putt, but Valeda sed we better lissen to that loud cracklin voice.

It tole us we hadda go blow back down all them stares and git on our puffed up vests. I minded that ther wuz a Teevee in our stately-room, and wen I tern it on it wuz givn us destructions on how to work the bellybands and underarms on our seebelts. The messedge cum in Anglish and then anuther langridge witch tern out to be Jermin . . . (no French or Jappaknee!) Then the cracklin voice tole us that we all hadda gather in yer big ballsroom up on Beedeck. I thot th' idee wuz to lern our station and how to git into them botes in case of murgensy, but insted the captin (or his mate . . . he's got

Overbord with the life bote drill

three of them!) tole us about all the helthy things we cud do on bored fer reckremation, like the Fit Nessenter and Airobix, and after we cood have a Sole Larium, a Sawna or a Jack Coozy.

Fer outsiders on deck ther wuz a Tomthum golfcorse with plasticle balls fer both yer driving and yer putz, and a gaim called Snuffelbord witch look like the plairs wuz moppin the dex. All this activititty they tride to git us into, insted of jist lettin us lain around enjoin ourselfs. The way the capting tocked we wuz in a float-in sitty. Ther wuz a bank, a Londer Et, a Haredressing bewdy saloon, a Lieberry, a Hospiddle, a Chapple, and a Sin-Agog.

After they tot us how to do up our casualty belts (witch we had allreddy put on in our cabbin) they had a loddery witch went with the numbers on yer shipstickits. Valeda figgerd I mite win agin with my Blotto Sex-Afore-Nine luck, but lowin' beehold it wuz the wife that wun this time. Two hunderd doller wortha bewdy treetment witch they garnteed wood take a cuppla inches offa her bellyband. She booked herself into that saloon fer the day before we wuz to land in Ire-land.

Speekin of bellybands, mine sure got straned to the limits on that see-goin trip. The best thing about yer Queenie Too is feedin' time witch kin happen five time a day and all fur free. I figgerd on gittin my munnys worth cuz after we git docked offa this ship the meels is all on me. So I deesided on a regler calorie stampeed. Furst, there's breckfust witch yiz kin have in 2 places . . . the one settin down at a tabel with all kindsa nivesinforks, and the tuther wuz at yer Leedo fer lader-getter-uppers, called a Buffoon Brunch, witch is wat they call breckfust witch you serves yerself, caffyteeria stiles. If a laid breckfust is brunch why don't they call tee-time lupper? The wife, hoo is partly diabolic, skipped this meel and insted went to our cabbin fer to fill herself fulla insolence. (Valeda is a vurry conshy-enshuss injector.)

I peefurred to sit down and git wated on. Our waders wuz two Anglish fellas, one a Yorky frum Leads, and the tuther a

Cocky frum Londin. They look after me like I wuz a hole tabel-fulla peeple, and gimmy a choice of porritch, 3 stiles of aigs, corny hash, kipper and finny haddy. I haddem all. Valeeda wuz into wockin round the deck to git reddy fer her bewdy treet-mints so she jist picked up brand muffins and yogart at the Buffoon.

Sumtimes I wuz the oney one of our tabel at breckfast. And the wether wuz perfeckly cam as the pam of yer hand. Not nice tho. As soon as we hedded out of yer Ewe Ass fer Novy Kosher and Newfyland we wuz doin' nothin' but duckin' the fog. Valeda had reserve us a cuppla deckschares and I sware we never got to use 'em the once.

Valeda becum offal edgy wen we got close to Stable I-land, named after all them unstable poneys roamin' around loose after all them shiprex. And next day she wuz jist as nervuss offa Cape Racey, Nofunland, ware that old fore-stacker yer Tye-tannick had bin ice-burged and sunked.

But back to the dinin' derangements. Wen the hole of our tablegang sat down together ther wuz sex of us, incloodin' a cuppla Noo Yawkers hoo tocked offal funny, and a married cupple frum Kaintucky hoo tocked jist as funny, yet all fore of them rored wen I sed my spouse seen a mouse about our house. The upshat of it all wuz that we figgerd that they figgerd we tocked jist as funny as we thot they did.

After lunchin' I figger why don't yiz go fer a troll on deck? But with all this fog ther wernt no seenery. Go inside and ther are lechers ware they show the moovys at nite, but most peeple seem to hang around them slut masheens. So I went back blow stares fer wat they call a post-randy-all nap. (Valeda sniffed and sez ther wuz lots to do in between meels, but her gut-fill-in hazbin wood wuz lyin in wate fer the nex call to the troff.)

Wunce I got woke up erly by a dubble bang frum the Conkurd plain flyin' over our heds, as it passed its moovemints thru wat they call yer SoundBarreller. (This jist meens that its

Sonnick booms went bust.) So I clum my way up to yer Beedex, and found that everybuddy had stop fer tee.

Tee-time had more kinda tees than I ever shook a spoon at: Url Gray, Cam-a-mile, Jardeeling, and Lopsy Shooshine. But the mane part wuz all kindsa gooey samwitches folleyed by cakes and tarts, and most speshully them scons cuvverd in strobbery jam and smutherd in that dubbled up creem maid by sum clots in Devvinsheer.

But the big meela the day wuz supper . . . wat they called dinner, and it wuz fancy dressed all the way, nuthin but yer best bib-bin tucker. It sed "black tie" on the Menyou but you hadda ware a coat and pants as well. I brung along my old Dad's tuck-seedoo, and the wife maid me a liddle dicky with a red boa tie on it to stick round my neck like a bib. Wuz I ever tuckerd by the time I got all drest like a pink sow fer markit.

After supper I hung around uptop insted of bein' smug in my bunk on accounta they advertize a Midnite Snatch. Fergit about sleepin pills, jist line up at that troff and pig out with the uther tenderloin nite riders. I tole yuh five, but

putrin on the dawg ta put on the feedbag

it wuz possibull to eet sex times a day on that bote! Cuz if yuh wuz shivvrin' in yer deckchare in all that fog, they pass around twice a day free cups of steemy gold bullion.

Deer Sun: The Hex mark on the tuthersidc of this postill card is ware we are cabinned. But I spend mosta my time in the dine-in room. Havin a wunderful time, wish you wuz her, cuz Valeda don't approove of all my goorman-dizing. (a goorman isa glutton that owns a dinner jacket.) Tonite they're throwin' Bake Alasker at us! Don't fergit to feed the stock — luv-yer stufft Dad

## Gail Farce, 10

The day Valeda went fer her two hunnerd doller bewdy treetment, I staid bunked digestin' the preeviuss days events, cuz I wuz fullern our silo frum last nite's midnite feest. Alluva sudden I got the shakes . . . I figgerd first mebby it wuz the aig-you, but it wernt me doin' the shakin, it wuz everythin elts in the cabin; the door cum offa the frigid-rater and iced coobs was all over the floor, and even the drores popped outa the burro ware we keep our close. I figgerd Valeda wood crick-etsize me fer cozzing this mess, serching franickly fer a fresh pare of undywares. But it were Muther Naycher's falt that our bedroom wuz goin up and down like yer Vancoover Sock Exchange.

I seen the waves splashin' all over our porehole! Insted of gittin up and cleenin up, I dun wat enny lanlubber wood do under them sircumstantses . . . staid in bed and cuvver up my hed. Valeda cum back frum her bewdy treetments all het up cuz they hadda stop before they finisht. They had slubberd her with bloogoo and rap her in seeweed like sum Japkneeze raw fish, (wat they calls yer squishy). She clames they had manedge to squeaze two inches offa her waste lines. But then they quit on her middel wen the bote started with yer rock'nroll.

Valeda wuz about to blow the whissle on me fer spreddin our close outa all the drores, and sprinkelin them with ice coobs, wen the uther wissle blew. It wuz time fer the lunch, cum helen hywater! So I grab my life-jackits and hed fer the dine-in room. Evenchly Valeda follied after. I dunno how she manedged with all them stares but I felt this time like I wuz climbing yer Matted Horn. I dunno wether it wuz yer ship's pitchin toss or my lacka eekwal-librium but I hadda take a side toor to the ships rale and settle my stummick in the Atlantical otion before per-seedin to the dine-in room.

Ther wuz a few uther harty soles had cum up to brave the elmints, and our 2 waders wuz ther to serve us. In fack we had a full tabel of sex. The waves wuz cummin up to the winder of our diner now, witch wuz 2 flores abuv our cabin, so them brakers hadda be at leest thurty-foot.

Heaving two

All thru the meel yude heer the tinkel of glass frum summers in the dinin' room. Ther wuz a yuge crockry crash on the tuther side of the room as our side of the bote went up hy and thairs went down low. Valeda, bean a Martimer, noo it wuz our tern next. She grab a wotter glass in eech hand and tole me to hang on to my plait. Shore enuff, our side went down as tuther side went up. I wuz push agin the tabel, but Valeda on the farside didden have no tabel to push agin, and she wuz throwed about thirty feet, landin rite agin the winder with the waves sloshin' about her. She still helled both them wotter glasses and I sware to hevvin she never spilt one drop. Yuh cant beet them seefairyin foke.

The captin cum on the entercum to tell us better we sat still ware we are, or go blow and git lade in our bunks. There wernt no more servicing us fer lunch so we figgerd we mite as well hed fer our cabbin. But we hadda stop and hold on to sumthing every few secunds. We went past the drinkin bar ware they had nitely ennertanemint, and the grand pianna had lost all its fore legs, and the base drum had a big hole in it on accounta sumbuddy had rolled acrost the flore and crashed intuit with his hed.

They say ther wuz thirty peeple injerd, but I never demand a recount. All I noe is the croo sed it wuz the biggest blow in five years. Winds wuz gale farce 10, and if ya gits to 12 it's a hoorovacane. The big bote keeled over to a angel of twenny three degree eether side. The most it had ever dun before wuz 25. So this oney happens wunce in a bloo moon. (Ackshully we found out later ther had bin a blue moon that nite, but nobuddy cood see it on accounta the wether.) I ast Valeda if she wood peefurr to fly home soons we landed. She give me sitch a look.

Nex day, the see wuz flattern pees on a platter, the sun cum out full, and all we cud see frum our porehole wuz the green hills of Ire-land. Witch is all we wanted to see. And I never seen sich green. Even greenern the faces of my fella passinjers the day before.

# Ire-land

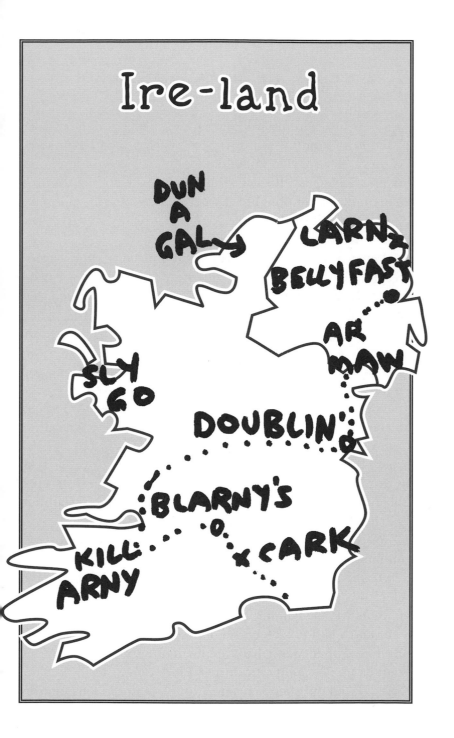

# Follying Our Ruts

As we cum close on Ire-land, it look like a pool tabel with smooth lumps. But it's a greener green than I ever seen. We wernt debarked at Cork like we thunk we wuz gonna be, but at a liddle coav. It's ackshully spelt like a corn cob with a aitch on the end (Cobh) but it's pernounce differnt, more like Coab or even Coav. (I had enuff trubble with my vowels in Ire-land without bringing up my continence.)

Watever it's call, it's a pritty liddle place, sorta a seaside reesort. We tuck a little fairy to git there. This is the place ware a lotta our pie-in-ear incesters started off fer Canda wen ther potaters terned black on them. It's also the place frum witch yer world's biggest bote, yer Tide-tannic, saled before meetin' up offa Newfyland with that ship-disturbin' iced burg!

Priddy as it wuz, the wife wanted to git offa yer Cobh and on to yer Cork fer to look up her famly tize. Cork is not jist a town, but it's also the countee town of yer countee of Cork, so Valeda figgerd the best way to look up her old fokes wuz at yer Countee Cork House. We tuck a buss to Cork, but not yer ornery buss, this hear wuz our toorbuss witch wuz gonna take us on to sites like rooned cassles, burried saints, blest statutes, holey mounds with Kiltick crosses, and a passle of Cathlick chirches fulla relicts open frum 9 to 5.

We wuz to take the saim buss on frum Ire-land acrost yer continence of Yerp, seven countrys in twenny daze. Valeda wuz nervuss about goin' thru that Chunnel funnel to Frants, but felt releefed wen she wuz tole it wuzn't open yit.

Sints we had commit ourselfs to bussin, Valeda oney had a our and a haff to look up her extinguished pre-dead-sessors. She found that mosta her peeple had cum frum Ar Maw, anuther Ire-ish county, up in per Proddestant north, but the wife did find out she wuz remoatly relate to the long-ded Erl of Cork, hoo wuz a Boyle on his father's side, and hoo invent sumthing call Boyle's law.*

There wernt no Drains in Cork, they wuz mostly in uther countys called Wecksford, or Waterfurt and in a liddle town called Ballymoney. Valeda wuz curios to find out ware all the Ballymoney in her famly went, but ther wernt time, cuz it wuz tooryist time. Sumbuddy bloo the wissle on us, so we hop abored the buss fer Barney's Cassle, jist up the rode aways.

> \* feat note: I figgerd the law wuz that Boyles brake out on yiz in sevens, but terns out to be sumthing about heeting worter to 212 deegreese Fattenheet, or a hunderd degheese Selfishness, and wen the steem cums outa yer keddle it's time fer tee.

Everybuddy that spoke Englitch around us on that bus seem to be talkin about "Kissin' Barney stoned." Valeda snift and sed she hadden cum all this way fer to git familyer with sum drug-taken purpull dinashore on the TV.

But we overheerd it rong. I dunno hoo got the ell outa there, but it wuz Blarney's Cassle we wuz at, and everybuddy wuz line up outside it fer to git to the top and leen over backerds fer to kiss his stones. Terns out Blarney wuz a Ire-ish lard hoo kep puttin' off Queen Lizzabath the Furst with sweetock wen it cum to doin fer hur wat he sed he'd doo. Anyways this name is now tide up with sayin' wat yuh don't meen, and ennybuddy hoo puts ther lips to his rocks qualifries to go into pollyticks.

This here cassle is a Middle-Evil Hy-rize that is compleatly uninhibited now eggsept by torryist gides and the two fellas that hold yiz by yer laigs five storys up wen ya bends over backerds. They lets yer head hang down undooley fer to kiss them cold slimed stones.

Altho' it fill Valeda with wunder, the flow-in streem beeside the cassle fill me with sumthin else, and I went lookin' fer a warshroom. I found it nex to yer Soo-Veneer senter, but the

Kissin'
Barney
stoned

sines on the two doors confuse me. Wun sed "M'na" and the tuther sed "Fir." I figger it wuz a tippical-graffical errer, but terns out to be the old-time Ire-ish langridge. I wuz about to go into yer "M'na" room, wen a women cum outa the door that I wuz about to cum in. By this time my back teeth wuz floatin' so I scurreed back to the cassle as fast as I cud with my laigs crost, and wen nobuddy wuz lookin', jist used the mote.

By the time I got back to the wife she wuz in a ring tail snorter of a fewry with me, on accounta the toor buss had gon on without us and taken our luggridge with them. The wife wuz absolootly beside hurself, witch I'm beginnin to think is her fave-rit posishun. There we wuz aloan and abandon in a forn country without a stitch nor a toothbrush!

# On the Rong Side of the Line

Valeda thot we cud catchup with them uther tooryists by takin' anuther buss, but I figger that wood leeve us allways a haff hour beehind it cuz these busses is all staggerd, (like Tooryists after a long hard day of tooristing). I look up the skedool and lern that our buss wuz gonna have lunch at a place call Durty Nellys, and dinner at a Bun Ratty cassle. A bunfeed in a ratty cassel didden sound too appytizen to me, and Valeda wernt too keen on meetin up with enny Durty Nelly, so I got suggestive about rentin a car fer a few ours. We cud git ahed of them tooryists, tern the car in, and wate fer our buss at a place witch sounded nice and restful neer a marsh called Mallow.

They didden have no Herz-to-Drive-yerself or even Rent-yer-Wreck, but ther wuz a Briddish cumpny called Yerpcar wood rant us a Ford Ex-Cort after we sined our life aways with a lotta sigmatures and nishuls on morn wun peesa paper. Valeda sat in the car wile I dun this. She thot she wuz in the passenger seet ware she allways sits wen we go to town. She notice that ther wuz a steer-in weel in frunta her, but she figgerd them Yerpeens had dum sum improovmints on backseet drivin' with duel controlls. But wen I got in ther wuz no steerin weel in frunta me, so I jist handed her the kees and tole her she mite as well drive.

She offen drives to town to sell her aigs wen I'm out with my Alice Chalmers. So I figgerd she'd be all dung-ho fer to hit the rode, and she thot the same till she almost hit a truck cummin on the saim side of the rode. He curse sumthin' in Ire-ish at her, and we figgerd he wuz drunk, till we found that all the other veehickles we met wuz drivin' on the rong side of the rode too, hunkin their horns at us like we wuz back in rush hour in downtown Nooyork Sitty.

Them Ire-ishers is so dang preverse that they all drives on the rong side a the rode. (I sposed it was to spike yer Briddish till I found out them Angled Sacksons do it too.) After Valeda got the hang of bein' in the rong, we started to injoy yer seenery. Ire-ish farms is reely neet . . . kinda like them on Prints Edwards Eyeland, ware yule never see a recked car sittin' on yer front lon. Everything wuz all so CLEEN, not a popboddle er a gumrapper in site, jist like yer Garding of Eeton musta bin.

It maid both of us wunder why our incesters ever left sich a plaice. (Ire-land I meen. We noe why our incesters left the Garden of Eaton's. They got kick out fer foolin around with sum Forbidding Fruit.)

By dinner time we had give up tryna overtook our tooryist buss, on accounta we had bin gittin lost in every nooky and granny. Even the mane rodes wuz offal narrer. Sumtimes weed squeeze past big trucks and almost scrape our sides.

But we enjoid gittin lost on yer Hy-ways and By-ways on accounta the seenery, and we kep gittin lost morn more the more we got direckshuns frum the lokels. Cuz frum the way they tocked Anglish it cudda bin a differnt langridge, and we shure wisht that they cum with sub-tittles. The both of us jist smiled at them and jestyerd thank youse, and then went heds first back into our rode map.

It wuz gittin on fer suppertime and Valeda wuz feelin her pangs morn usual sints she had tuck a cuppla inches offa her bellyband on bored ship. She thot we shood stop in the town of Noomarkit (sounded to us like back home Ontaryio) at a nice liddle old pubic house call Skully's. It tern out to be wat the Irish call a snug, or a shebeen, ware they all drinks pot-sheen* but most of the inhibitants wuz drinkin sum blackstuff with a creemy top. Tern out to be Ginny's Stout.

> \* firnote:
> Home-bruise, like screechin' shine, or even wite litening.

Despike the odd laps on this trip, Valeda claims she is strickly Temprunce and she snift offensivly wen the first thing they ast her wuz if she wanted to git stout. She orderd a limonaid and the pubelican sed with a twinkie in his ize "White or red?" and everybuddy lafft. She bridel a bit and order insted a potta tee with her samitches, and everybuddy laffed agin. They brung it to her in a liddle brown pot, but they musta put sumthing elts in it, cuz within ten minits she wuz singin' "Gall Away Bay" to her hart's contempt.

Valeda has tea-total

Valeda is mickeyfinned and it soots her to a tea

# Amung Yer Long Villains

It wuz time fer "Time!" in that pubelick house, so we all got up and went. It wuz then I reelize we didden have a plaice fer to lay our heds that nite. But a yung fellow nex to us drinkin his glassa port sed that his mum had a bedden breckfust plaice at witch he wuz the cook. Enny glass a port in a storm I figgerd, so we folleyed him home, this time me at the weel on the rong side of the rentle car. We wuz tuck to a regler manshin on mebby five hunnert akers of land. No argymints frum us that time a nite, so we wuz hussle upstairs to a reel fetherbed with a canopee over it, insted of under like back home.

Our furse nite in Ire-land Valeda and me slep like the ded in that fethery bed, till well passed choretime nex day. We jist got down in time fer the last call fer breckfust served by the cook's Mum, Jane-o Callyhan. Her place is called "Longvill." and yer Callyhens lost it morn three hundert yeers ago to that Anglish Overlard and Pooritanickle Protecter, Allover Crumwell. I gess he's the Long Villen the house is naim after. Them Callahens oney got it back a few yeer ago, and bed'n breckfust has becaim their bred'n butter.

Nobuddy duz it better I bet. They had appeljooce frum their own apples, and fresh ruebarb frum the garding. A Ireish breckfust has more things on ther plaits than we got. Along with yer bakin' and aigs is livers and kid-knees, and sumthin' called sody bred, witch must be wat gives Ire-ishmen a jet-propel jumpstart in the morning.

We wuz both so blaim full of it, that the wife and former sweetart and I went back to bed till dinnertime (noon) instedda of seein' the lo-cal sites, or tryna catch up with our tooryist buss. As I wuz on the way back upstares after breckfus to "kip" agin (have a knap) I seen about haff a duzzen big sammon line there in the foy-yeah (frunthall) on a plait had jist bin cot fresh in yer Blackwotter River. Sez Jain "That's fer tee!" (supper). Valeda and I look at eech uther and figger on stain a extry nite.

I never et so gud in all my borned daze, inclooding the "horses doovers" (iddy biddy snatches of fud) in the liberry in frunt of a roring fire. Valeda had the sammon and I went fer sum lam, both rezzdents on the premmisses so to speek, and after that we got our just desserts. Sum liddle cakes called in French "petty force," and then, as the old sayin goes, Valeda had her truffles and I had mine witch wuz rolled in coco and fresh ornj peels. Then we had a razzberry coolus (Ire-ish fer a moose) with liten dark choclit. I went to bed stufft and dremt of that turble fam-in that maid my famly leeve this tooryist Pairadice. Mebby if us Farquharsons had staid heer we'd be livin to eet insted of jist eetin to live.

# Rode to Dubblin

Sints all my four fathers cum frum yer North, and sum of Valeda's fokes wuz also Boarderline cases frum up Ar Maw way, we deesided to hit the rode fer Bellyfast by waya Dubblin hopin' we cud ketchup with our busstoor frum there. Valeda

wuz use to sittin' on the rite-hand side (wat yer Axident pre-
venshun peeple calls the deth seet) so she tuck the weel agin.

First of all we went a cuppla miles to the bustop in Mallow on
Valeda's hunch, and rite enuff she was, fer ther wuz a note
address to a Mistern Miz Charleen Farkyouharson sayin' "See
you In Dublin!" But no sine of our luggridge. Valeda side and
bot sum washpowder fer to do up her smalls and my bigs.
So we set off fer Dubblin fer to ketch up with our fella
tooryists, but with me reedin the map we got lost agin. They
got cloverd-leefs over here but they calls them roundy-bouts
and I kin see why, cuz the sines leedin to them are offal confuze. I heer storys about peeple with three days growth a beerd
spendin overnites on them blaim things. They have reststops
called lay-buys fer yiz jist to ponder yer wandrins. Mine jew,
we didden mine gittin lost too much, cuz we found ourselfs
goin' thru the laiks of Kill Army. The landescape look like a
combynation of Swishyland and our B.B.C. (Bewdyful Birdish
Clumbya) oney the hills wernt vurry high. They seem to reelize that cuz ther called the Boggerall Mountings.

Valeda clames she got us to Dubblin's fare city under her
own steem, but she wuz pritty steemed by the time we got to
yer Hy-Burner-ya, witch is not a oiledfeeld underwater in
Newfunland but a bran new Hotel reckamend by the rental-
car peeple. The wife had had enuff not seein' the seenery, but
ther'd be no more drivin' fer Valeda ennyway, cuz we cooden
take the car acrost that boarder into Bellyfast. Sumthin bout
Ire-ish pounds bean different frum Anglish pounds. So we turn
the car in before we turned in and turned our toes up that nite.

Nex mornin I look up yer Dubblin fonebook. Ther wuz
lotsa funny naims, Loobys and Looneys and a cuppla Feerys,
and miles and miles of Boyles, but ther wuz also nine
Farquharsons. I never tole Valeda about that rash of Boyles, cuz
I wanted to git on to my peeple in the Ulsterd North. But wile
she wuz on the throan I rang the odd Farquharson. Nobuddy
wuz home so I left a massage.

First place Valeda wanted to go to wuz the Dubblin Post Office, but I tole her that wuz ware all them Ire-ish trubbles began. She sed we got the saim problims back home, but she wuzzen awair that over here back in 19-ot-16, their Post Office end up in rebellyun. Besides, I wuz gittin hungered agin, so I tocked her into sum fission chips. After that we walked all over Graftin Street becuz its strickly fer pederastrians.

We had sich good mammarys of that liddle pub in Noomarkit, we deesided to try Dubblin nite life. It didden tern out that good. Ther was morn one old soddin fella sittin outside a pub with his hed in his hands and lookin the worse fer ware. Valeda snift and felt the licker laws wuz too loose fer her taist.

The pub wuz jam to the dores and it tuck a wile fer us even to git neer the mewsick plairs. Ther wuz a bandjoe, a mandleinn, a vile inn that never got plaid, a geetar, a Ire-ish baggedpipe (a liddle thing compair to yer Scotsbrand, looked more like a dust-buster) and lots and lots of pints of Ginnys consonantly bean refilld by a liddle gurl hoo look no more than thirteen. She also brung samwitches, oney a few of witch got eeten, but lodes and lodes of drink was past down gullits. Ther wuz a big argymint tween the bandjoe and the geetar as to hoo wuz in toon, and the geetar started to git a bit nasty and he still had three Ginnys to go. We left before a fite started and hed back to our huttel.

Erly nex mornin I wuz awokened by a Dubblin Farquharson naim Robbin, with hoom I had left a massage the nite before. He tern out to be the lokel clanhed, and a bit of a histerian, so I ast him to cum and have a cuppa tee before we tuck the trane. He tole me his buncha Farquharsons cum frum a place in the center Hylands of Scotland neer Pitlockry called Dull. But they got cleered out by the Sassynackers (Anglican Sacksons) and went to Eddinburg, then cum over to Dubblin durin a bildin boom and staid ever sints, but with no reegrets—Pressedbyteerians in a Cathlick hot bed.

Robbin felt the Berdish guvmint wuz gittin fed up with spendin billyums of pounds on the trubbles in North Ire-land. He also sed if I wuz lookin fer my ruts, I wuz in the rong place. Scotland is the real berthplace of our clan. Wen I say "clan" I don't mean them hoods in the starch bedsheets with the pointy heds, yer Kooky Klutzers. I meen the bunch frum witch all of our famly is deesent frum time in memoriam. This Robin had bin to see yer Farquharson of Farquharsons over to Bray Mar Cassle, and he advice me I shood go there to stir up my ruts. He didden think ide find menny Farquharsons in Bellfast cuz mosta them had emmygrated to Tronto!!

# Bellyfast

Deer deer Letitia:

How did the meeting of the WCTU go? We spent last nite in a gin-soked pubic house in Dubblin that wood make even those See Grim peeple take the pledge. I haven't cum across any of our Boyle kin yet, but Charles wants to get on to Belfast where his blood lies. Take care. We will.

Your cousin Valeda.

I dunno exackly wen we crostover to the northern side of Ireland cuz ther were no checkpoints Charlie on that train. Valeda writ a buncha postcards to all them cussins back home hoo had tride to mooch munny frum us, and she put Airy-ish (suthern) stamps on them. Witch don't hold acrost yer boarder ware they have the Queen's Hed on them like we do. We hadda tip the stewyass on the train to take our cards back and male them frum Dubblin. So alreddy we wuz feelin their differences.

Alluva sudden things looked more industreel . . . less greenry and more red bricks and smoky stax . . . mebby more Briddish. It shure felt like a differnt country frum wat we had cum frum in the deep south of Ire-land.

We tole the gabby driver to take us to yer best Bellfast hotel. (You oney live wunce by the Blotto 649!) He tuck us to yer Yeroper . . . witch we lader found out had the most bommed reckerd in Ireland. (Not the cussdummers, the hoetell.)

We got up to our room offal tired and orderd ourselfs to be room serviced, witch meens they brings the fud to yer dore. It wernt long in cumming but wun slurp of soop and Valeda turn green, went into the barfroom, and woop her cookys. Tock about yer Bellyfast, the wife never et anuther bite all the time we wuz there.

She went to bed rite away but cooden git cumferbull, so she took all her bedclose and pit them on the flore and in no time I herd a snore. There wuz no way us Farquharsons wood be on the town that nite, so I started lookin' up naims in the fone book. I got a shock. Ther wuz oney 3 Farquharsons list in the hole sitty! But ther wuz 38 Drains, 70 Harrons, and 2 McKinnons. So I got into yer Drains, and found that the wife cum frum a long line of Huge Nuts, (witch is French fer Proddestint) hoo got kick out of Fran's fer not bean Cathlick (them as wernt massacreed by sum Saint Barf-all-amuse). It seems that them Frenchdrains wuz the best ther wuz that got tide up in the lacy bizness, and it wuz them start up the big traid heer in Ire-ish lace. So that's how Valeda's bunch happen to git to be Ire-ish lace-ists.

We never did git down to Ar Maw fer to check on Valeda's partickler Boyls, fer the wife threw up all our plans fer to visit the Mountings of Morn, and yer Gigantic Cozzway, and jist lay on her side on the huttel flore, dubble up in yer fatal posishun.

Nex day I book passidge on the fairy to Scotland, and spent the resta the time in a taxee-cab lookin' at the lokel sites both Proddestant and Cathlick. The wife lay on her bed of pane, gittin' up oney to throw up and do our nitely londry in the uther base-in on accounta our clothes wuz still ahed of us on root to summers elts.

The room clark at the huttel sed ther wuz rank taxees outside the bildin. I sed I wuz hopin' fer wun that smelt fresh but he didden seem to noe wat I wuz tockin about. I snift out the first cab and it seem to smell o.k. The driver's name wuz Shame-Us, and I ast him to take me to the Wore Zones. He tole me it wuza kinda erly fer them wores to be up. It tuck me a wile fer to unnerstand he wuz tockin about worehouses. I tole him I wanted to see the meen streets ware ther wuz all the trubbles between yer Prod and yer Cathlick. He laffed a lot, and sed he dout if ther wuz much goin' on, but heed take me to see all the muriels on the walls in both yer Falls (Catlick) and yer Shankill Rodes (us Prods).

He tuck me furst to yer Shankle Rode witch he sed wuz libel to have sines tellin' the Pope in so menny words "to go forth and multiply hisself!" I wuz glad Valeda wernt on bored but we never seen one. They musta bin all scrub out by yer IRAtes in the middla the nite. They had one muriel of the Pope holdin' up a Orange scarf with Ulcer on it. Shame-us sed that wuz sumbuddy's ideer of a joke and he showed me anuther sine sayin' "No Popery Here!" (I allus thot popery wuz the dride flours Valeda stuffs in our drawers every fall fer to make our undys smell sweet all winter.)

I seen morn one big millinery fort with barb wire up to the top flores. Shamus jist laff about it. He sez the pleece like to have wall ta wall barbwire like we has brod looms. It's hard to tell wen Ire-ishmen is seerious or not. The Prottestants say the

NOotered in the middel

sityation there is seriuss, but it's never hopeless. The Cathlicks say it's hopeless but never seeriuss. I figgerd Shame-us fer one of them Catlick Micks. He admit it.

So I ast him to take me to see his side a the street. He didden have to drive morn a step . . . jist kep on yer Donnygal Rode and the saim street terns into wat the Gaylick sine sed wuz Sraid DunNa n Gall (Dunnygal Rode to yoon me). Both sides wuz sharin' the same rode, livin' cheeks by ther jowls! We went up yer Falls Road, and seen the Cathlick muriels. Ther all fresh lookin, not painted over frum yeers ago. Ther mostly frum the last ten yeers, and the only time they gits extry paint on them is wen the Proddestants sneek in at nite and throw paint bottles at them. Shame-us sez Cathlick muriel painters expeck that, and feel gud about it, cuz they figger they're own partickler poppy-gander is reely makin its effeck. Both sides feechers a lotta mask men in ballyclavvers with Oozy masheen guns.

I ast Shame-us if the killin wood ever end. He sez it's goin' thru the changes. Yer Shin Fame (plitickle part of yer I.R.Ates) has now got a majorty on the Bellfast Sitty Counsel so there goin in morn more fer votes than feelin ther otes. But the neecappin goze on, he sed. "Wat's that?" sez I. Seems it's a way to mame sumbuddy without terminatin' ther life. They put a gun to the back of yer leg, or yer arm or yer elboe,and it terns yiz into a live crippel. It started with yer Shins Faners doin' it to ther infarmers, but it's now became jist as common amung

Gettin' plastered against a Muriel

Proddestant Parry-miltrys hoo take the law into ther own jurysdiction. In fack us Prods is now nummer one on the Hate Prade, 39 mirders to 30 frum yer IRAtes.

But a lotta the miner crimes is being commit by teeny agers hoo dont blong to eether side. Jist hell-razors on ther own. Seems ther's not too much respeck fer Lawn Order, and the yung hoods hoo got nuthin' to do with eether side of the polltickle streets is runnin' a muck. A lotta them joy-ridin' joovy niles deelinkwents wuz tot how to steel cars frum gun-min on both sides. But now, the yung are freelansers hoo do it jist fer kix. And they even compeets with eech uther fer havin the biggest scars frum ther neecaps as a kind of Mawcho badge of onner! No wunder Ulcer's biggest export is peeple. Mosta the Arsh peeple I nose in Canda is refuge-jeez frum this place.

We druv acrost the Rivver Laggin into Eest Bellyfast, the industerearial parta town, fer to see the biggest crains in the wirld. I thot they'd be mebby like pink flamin-goes on wun laig, but these is yer dry-doc cranes, much biggern that. This wuz the biggest ship bilding rig in the wirld, but Shame-us tole me it wuz offal hard fer a Catlick to git a job in that shipyard. He sed it wuz jist relijuss racy-ism, and not becuz Popers like him wuz consider to be trubble-makers. And jobs is gittin' scairce anyways. He blaims the trubbles in Northern Ireland on yer Japa-knees. I didden understand till he sed that Toke-yo and Yoke-a-homo undycuts Bellfast and makes the saim ships biggern fastern cheeper. Shamus called it Jappa-kneescapping.

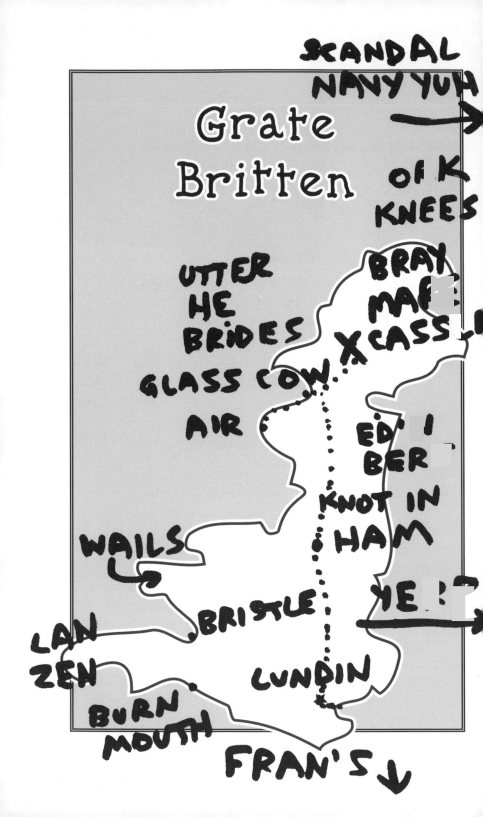

# Scots Wa Hae, Haw!

Valeda wuz still feeling peely-wally (Scots fer pukey) wen we left Bellyfast that afternoon. I kep Shame-us on fer to take us to the porta Larn, a pritty farlarn lookin' plaice witch wuz ware we wood bored the fairy fer Scotland. He tole us on root that we never got to see the pritty parts of Ulcer (like them tooryists on our mist bus!) and we shooda gon up yer Gigantic Cozzway with its volcanical larva soliddyfied into 40,000 base-salt colyums, or we cooda shot strait up yer Antrim, fer to see the lakes of Ballymeany. But Valeda wuz feelin' too bleery-ide and ballymeany herself fer to see sitch sites. I wuz worried about gittin' her acrost yer Norse Chanel of yer Ire-ish See without a hole-scail evackyouation, but Valeda sed wen it cum to her stummick she had nuthin' but bile left. Sounded like the trubbled land we wuz jist leevin.

In ackshell fack, I needna worried about Valeda's passidge. That bote trip frum Ire-land to Scot Land wuz jist as cam as yer P.I.E. Fairys goin' frum Cape Turpentime to Boredom. I never found if they had clan chowder fer sail, cuz Valeda lay with her hed in my lap all the way acrost frum shore to shore with a peecefull snore.

By the time we got to Stan Rare, (Stanraer) witch wuz the end of our jurny, she wuz feelin pert neer purky. We had hope to run into the inhibitants of our tooryist buss on the trip over, but we wuz both unmobile on accounta Valeda's hore-zontal-ness so weel never noe if they wuz abored. But ther wernt no buss at the end of the Scots pee-er so we figger we musta mist conneckshuns agin. This ment we hadda keep on warshing out our unmenshunables every nite instedda steppin into cleen close, witch wuz still (we hoped) on that blaim runnyway buss. I figgerd we shood fergit about chasin after our close now that we wuz in the incestral homeland, and mebby git ourselfs tartanned up a bit. Valeda felt that plad undyware mite run in the warsh-basin. But I figger wunce ya gits used to travellin without luggridge . . . and stairin' down the hoetell staffs . . . it beets hawling around mountins of Samsumites. I wanted to hed strait fer the incestral home of the Farquharson clan . . . Bray Mar Cassel. The Travvle fella in the bust deepoe attach to yer Fairy sed that no toor busses went all the way up yer Hy-lands frum his parts, so best I rent-a-car agin. Valeda shudder, more at the thot of my map reedin than her drivin, but ther wuz no alturdnative. So we went to yer Anus rentacar bunch ("WE STRAINS HARDER") and they loned us a Anglish car. It wuz called Rover, reel smart lookin, and naim after sumbuddy's dog, I spose.

The rode strait north frum yer Fairy Terminable wuz along the seecoast and reemind us of the Martimes roundybouts Mahome Bay . . . But jist like in Ireland, we kep gittin the runaround frum all them roundybouts they has. All the sines seem to point the rong waze and it wuz like a maze to git back on the rite track, and we also run into lotsa deetoors and dee-virgins (that meens yuh can't cum in).

First stop we maid wuz the liddle villedge of Alloway. We mite a not stopt, eggsept I seen the cottedge by the rodeside with a sine that tole us inside wuz borne the grate Scotched Poe-it Rabbi Burns. This wuz ware he kep his butt, ben, and bire till he wuz past sex yeers old. He lader grew up to be a faled farmer. No wunder he's the wife's faverit, cuz her own hazbin's in the same bote. Rabbi wuz also consider to be a unsivvle servint, but a sucksessful rake.

I had brung along my old Glum-Garry hat frum the Parry Sound Pipe Band (I wuz thurd burd-whissle frum the reer) and got Valeda as offishul fornographer to flash her browny as I wuz ree-siting Burn's pome "To A Louse." That's me electro-cuting the part ware he writ "Wee sleekit cowrin' timrous beestie, o wat a panick's in thy brestie!" The wife sez I got the wrong pome . . . it's pernounce "To a Moose" . . . but by

Declaimin'
Rabbi
Burns

BURNS COTTAGE
Robert Burns the Ayrshire poet
was born in this cottage
on the 25ᵀᴴ Jan. A.D. 1759
and died 21ˢᵀ July A.D. 1796 age 37½ years.

swinjer, I never seen one of them big horny devils fittin' that tiny prescrip-shun.

After Alloway we got as far as Air, the senter of Burns country. Burns is consider the father of his country round these parts, partly on accounta his pomes and learyicks, but mostly on accounta he sired eleven ill-ledge-intimate children, but oney two pares of twins to speek of. No wunder he dide erly of a ruemantical hart condishun.

# You Tack the Low Rode, Weel Hit the Hy Rode

On the rode agin, the wife kept chaffing me fer stickin my face in the map and missin all the rode sines on the roundybouts. But I cooden take my eyes offen this map, becuz of all the familyer places that sound the same as we got back in Canda . . . Abbotsford, Ailsa Craig, Angus, Banff, Biggar, Calgary, Callander, Campbelltown, Clyde River, Craigellachie, Devil's Elbow, Duncan, Dundee, Dunstaffnage, Fort William, Glengarry, Hamilton, Ingonish, Keppoch, Kildonan, Lanark,

Lauder, Lowther, Maitland, (New) Glasgow, Paisley, Perth, Preston, Rockliffe, Rothesay, Saint Andrews, Selkirk, Stewart, Stirling, Stornoway, Strathearn, Tantallon, Thornhill, Tobermory, Tweed, Wick.

Scotland felt vurry much like home to both us Farquharsons after we got north of Glass Cow. On our way up to yer Hy Lands ther wuz a lotta fur trees and it look jist like our Muss-koker. Wen we got into yer Crampian hills, they wuz snowed on top. After the lushes of Ire-land, this land-escape look more bleek and barn, like our Articks. The big thing that wuz missin wuz yuman beans. The popillation seem to be mostly unnacumpaneed sheep and lams, not a visibull live-in breeth-in Scot in the lot.

Wen we got to Bray Mar up yer Deeside it wuz a bit more inhibited. Accorn to the rode sine, the town had mebby two hunnert peeple in it, and wuz list as a skee reesort, but we wuz gittin on fer worm wether. Yer Mitchell-inn Gidebook sez that the bigggest thing goin on is yer Braymar Hyland Gaims, first weak in September. That's wen them two hunderd has to squeeze in morn twenny thousand peeple!

The town (villedge reely) wuz fulla Sue Veneer shops, sum of witch sold home-maid tartins, kilts, sporns, (the big hairy-thing hangin down yer frunt) and even a skin-doo witch is the jerk ya puts in yer sox, (a nife at yer nees in case of fudes, but by now mostly serry-moany-all). Valeda bot sum undy-things that nobuddy wuz ever gonna git to see, cuz she wuz tired of her nitely dippins. I went hole hawg fer the Farquharson kilt and sox and a tammy shatner—yer Scots tam with a chairy on top.

Before hittin' on Braymar Cassle, a haff a mile away (mind, the Scots mile is longern yer Anglish mile, gives ya more fer yer munny . . . ha ha) we figgerd we better git dug-in fer the nite. (Dugs is a werd they use over heer fera place fer to stay over.) We seen a sine sed Braymar Lodge, so we lodged there. Terns out it had bin a shoot-in lodge fer the old-time

Farquharson lards fer wen they wuz feelin gamey and in season.

We wuz lucky to be lodgers at the Lodge cuz it wuz run by a hamsom yung cupple frum Abnerdean hoo had never run into eech uther till they met skeeing in yer Hosstrian Halps. Fer starts on our supper ther wuz what they called Scot Pro-Shoot-o, witch wuz vennyson cut thin as tiletpaper and serv with mellinballs. The mane corse wuz sammon with aigplant and taters, all maid in hevven, folleyed by dessert call Ath-hole Broze. It wuz a kind of wisky oatmeel in creem sprinkel with fresh jinjer. It look like vaniller moose but with more kick. After that ther wuz oncy wun place to go. Bed. Fer wun thing I wuz startin to git a sniffel frum waring my kilt the propper way. . . . nuthin' on under it but my shooze and stockins. Valeda sez I musta got cot in a draft. I dunno ware it cum frum, but I shure noo ware it wuz goin. Breckfust wuz in frunt of a roring fire. (More ded trees bein cremated fer to keep the wife and I in heet!) Poach aigs on smokey haddock and fresh scoans with home-maid Marma Laid.

This wuz erly in the mornin, and we wanted to git a crackadawn start fer our toor of Farquharsonland. But as soon as we open the door of our rent-a-Rover the sireen went off like to

Takin' a sheepish look at Scotland

waken the ded. If anybuddy wuz sleepin in after seven o'clock they shure got a rood awakening call. Valeda don't think we'll ever git the nerves to cum back this way agin. Wen the offal whale dyed down we fled to Braymar Cassel, the seet of my incesters.

# Deep in My Ruts

We wuz erly fer the openin' of the Farquharson Cassle. It's a tooryist detraction now, with regler offiss ours, and the Laird hisself lives a Scotsmile away in his spair cassle at Inferacold. (Witch is morerless wat I wuz feeling.) Braymar Cassle is a itty bitty of a thing compair to yer Buckinghams or even yer Balls Morals. Jist a nice lordly country home with a buncha turts, and no mote, but a ten feet wall to keep out evaders.

The Cure-Raider of the Cassle (cared-taker in charge) cum along about nine a'clock and let us in. Sints we wuz the furst fer the day, and my naim is Farqhuarson, we got a gran toor pursnally direckedted by Alec Callander, hoo wuz cheef gilly* to our hed Farquharson.

Furst thing Alec tole us wuz that this cassle wuz not the orignal. It got burn down back in 1698 by a wildman call Blackjack Farquharson. Valeda ast how cum a Farquharson bern down a Farquharson cassle? This kind of arson around didden seem to make too much cents to me eether. But we wuz tole that this heer Brae Mar at that time wuz the home of the Farquharson's sworn enema, Erl of Mar, hoo bilt it as yer bullwerks agin the powers of the Farquharson clan. That's why Blackjack Farquharson got to be so revolting, and sloo yer Erly Mar rite

* Feartnote: Nuthin fishy about him. He wuz a indenchured servint witch meens he had all hiz own teeth.

in his own dore-way (ware we wuz even now standin!) and slep with his widder that nite!!! Valeda look at me sidewaze wen she herd I cum frum a long line of blag-gerds the like of that. Seems my incester wuz quite a carcter, use to summon his servints to cum cleer his tabel, not by ring-ing his bells, but lettin off a pistle shot. I wuz beginnin to be sorry the wife wuz along wen I found out wat had cum before in my fambly.

Jist as we wuz leevin' yer Braymar Cassle we got a luvly sprize. Wile we wuz rubberneckin' the cassle Alec had fone up the currant Farquharson of Farquharsons, the rainin Laird at Invercauld Cassle, Captin Alwyn Compton-Farquharson (a ossifer in yer Scotsgrays, hoose pipers dun that Amazin Graze reecord). He wuz cummin over to pay us his respecks. His hed gilly, Alec, had tole us that the Captin had jist bin married, and wuz jist over a big party with his tenance on the ile of Mull, ware he mates Hyland Caddle. Valeda felt we shood giv him sum kind of a weddin presence.

He druv up jist as we cum outa the cassel, so Valeda greet him with a song fer to sellabate his marge. I wuz hopin' she'd sing "Will Ye Noe let us back in agin," but she dun sumthin' in a forn langridge. It all sound Sweetish to me, but the laird seem to unnderstan every word. He wuz all smiles wen he let me have my pitcher took with him and then tuck off in his Benchly car (witch is first cussin to yer Roles Roist).

After he left, I ast Valeda wat wuz the song she sung to him. She sed she never noo wat the gay Lick words ment but the name of the toon wuz yer Riskay Luv Learicks.*

\* NOTE: Erriskay Love Lyrics

# The Hart of the Umpire
## (Creckshun: Yer Cuminyerwelth)

We drop the car off in Glasgow and book raled passidge to Lundintown. Valeda and me both think them Briddlish tranes is the bees nees, cuz yuh gits to hav yer own apartment, and peeples drops in wunce in a wile to reed ther papers and git off wen ther time cums. They don't seem to wanna communitycate with ennybuddy excep with ther paper. Fine with me.

Ther wuz lots to look at out the winder as we wuz wizzin past three thousand yeers of histry. The wife wanted to make sure we hitched up with that busstour that we mist back in Ireland. I tole her this hole trip seem to be "chase-the-buss after our undyware." She glaired back and sed that wernt wat we wuz doin' in Scotland . . . "We wuz lookin up YER Ruts!" She's jist jellus she aint got no Scotch in her blud.

The wife on yer other ham, wuz into her litry world. We passed thru York Sheer, and she kep tellin' me about them Bronky sisters puttin on ther Jane airs and climbin ther withering hites to go fer a tramp across amoor. She kep wishin' we cud git to Strapford-a-Knavin' fer to see on stage sum of Shakespeer's parts. Myself, I'd like to of seen that round table they had fer all them nites in the cassel of King Arfer's Came A Lot. But Valeda felt so close to our cleen close she sed she cud smell them.

First thing we do wen we gits to Lundin is fone up the busstoor peeple and git aholt of our luggridge. There's a red-fone booth jist outside the trane station. I dunno how yer sposed to heer on yer uther end with all them pederastrians goin by. Lundin has more streetpeeple than Scotland and Ireland put together ain't got.

Valeda glairs at me stairing at all this and pints to the fone. She figgers if we cood conker the drivin over here, weer reddy to tackel ther tellyfones. But before ya cood say Grame Bell we wuz more confuze than we ever wuz on ther rodes. First of all I gotta look up the buss cumpny in the fonebook. They got morn wun!! I meen fonebooks, not bustcumpnys. In fack ther's a hole passel of fone books jist fer this wun sitty! I got the wife to go thru sum of the books wile I pour thru the uthers. Took us best part of a haff hour fer to find the dam nummer. But that ain't haff the baddle. First we trys to sorts out how much munny they wants fer yer input. We found out them coin sluts dont take Irish munny but they'll settle fer Scotch. Our travelling agent tole us back home that the Briddish has dessimated therselfs from yer LSD, witch is what they use to call ther pounds, shill-ins and pants. Now they tell me it's fer simple peeple, cuz there's a hunderd peas to yer pound. We had borried a outa date gide book frum Wirld War eleven, so wen Valeda tride to git on the fone, it was easy fer her to get cot with her pence down, and nowadaze there's no farthing around.

Then we gotta figger out witch button on the fone fer to press, yer A or yer B. They got destructions print in the frunta the fonebook, but they're jist as confuze as I am by this time.

The wife finely tuck charge and she got thru. Wen she finely got them busstoorers on the line (don't ast me how) she cood heer them, but they cooden heer her. Valeda thot it wuz all the streetnoise outside a the station, but she had fergot to press one of them fool buttons. Sumbuddy passin by seen we wuz in trubbles and stop to help. He push more buttons so the wife could make herself herd and she finely got a disemboddy voice that give her yer Bustoorers address at sum Sirkus called Pickyer Dilly.

Our noofound frend tride to give us dreckshuns but this fella had wat Valeda sed wuz a Cocky axent. Watever it wuz I cooden hardly unnerstand a syllabub of wat he wuz sayin'. Eggsept fer a cuppla wirds . . . "Tike a tyube! . . . Pick A Dilly!" I had no ideer fer wat perpuss we shood pick sum dilly of a toob.

This cocky fella pointed to a hole in the ground witch tern out to be yer intrance to a slubway like they has in Trauma. A sine sed Undyground and the fella sed it run all under the hole of yer sitty. Valeda wuz relucktant to lower herself, and wen she seen a bus go by with the wirds "Pick A Dilly Sirkus" she woop with joy and wuz determin that werever we wuz goin, it'd be overland, and not thru yer Undyworld.

Our Cocky frend sed the busspeeples address wuz nex door to that Serkus in Pickyerdilly. I wuz wondrin' wether it had three rings and ellafants wen Valeda thank him, grab me and drug me abored wun of them red busses. The ground floor wuz full so we hadda go up in the attick. I'm not serprize they have to dubble up on ther busses over here, on accounta ther vast copulation.

We wuzn't ther two minits before sum conducker cum up top with us and shouted at us "Fair Spleeze!" We didden noe wat he wuz tockin about, so he tole us fer to git offa the buss. We finely give up and tuck a tacksee over to yer Pickyer Dilly Sirkus. But it musta fold up its tense and left town. That tacksee tuck us rite to the Tooryist offiss and we fine to our dizzmay that our hole crue had jist left fer Amsters Dam! This wuz acrost yer Chanel in Haw Land! The fella beehind the desk tole us they got two Dutch artists muesleums to visit there, yer Rem Bran and yer Van Go, so he figger they'll be ther at leest two daze.

That give us 1 day in Lundin fer to do all the sites. We had to choose, cuz there's so blaim menny . . . Nummer wun fer Valeda wuz yer Bucking Ham's Paliss. She wuz hopin' to git inside the grounds after payin' her fifteen bucks like the resta them tooryists but that wooden happin yet fer a cuppla munths wen them Roils all went on ther summer vocations up yer Ballsmorals. So the wife'd have to be satisfride with standin on the outside by yer senchury boxes and gittin' a peak at them Coldcream gards in their bareskins going thru the changes Next on Valeda's wishlist wuz Ma Damn Two Sods whackswirks. The wife still cant bleeve they put up a John Majer and tuck down a Marg Snatcher.

My list wooda inclood Nummer Tent Drowning Street, then hop acrost to the Muther of all Parlmints in yer Common House a Lards, then look up at yer Big Bends fer to check on the creck Greenwitches meen time, and mebby spend ten minits in yer West Minister's Abey fer to checkoff the well-noan dead. But lastly, yet mostly of all, I wanted to git to yer Towering Lundin! Not to see them London Britches falling down (they wernt), but fer to vue morn nine hunnert yeers of bluddy histry ware a lotta big names got the axe frum the Guvmint cutbacks.

# Towering Lundin

Wen it cum to toorin' towerin' Lundin nex morn Valeda and me sets off in oppsit direckshuns fer to fill our wills. That sounds offal terminal. I jist ment we went our seprit waze fer to look up our own partickler sites. I felt in my boans that the hollyday Valeda reely needed wuz to be away frum me fer a bit.

She tole me later she seen yer Quean's own Household Calvary in frunta the Bucking Hampaliss, as they wuz droppin ther horseballs after cumming outa yer Quean's park, witch is divide in two parts and is called Hide, Sin James. Them horesmin cum upon her alluva suddin and Valeda hadda run outa ther way in a one woman Calvalry stampeed.

But she never got furthern the frunt door of Ma Damn Two Sods, cuz she ast direckshuns frum the doreman and he refuze to anser her. She went away blaim mad, but found out lader he were made of whacks. Then she cooden find eether Wimpydon or yer old Curio shop, so she end up goin to the Reejints Pork Zoo ware she seen a buncha chimp pansys havin hy tee, and havin a hy old time doin it. Valeda sed she neer wet herself laffin at ther ant ticks. Then she went shoppin up Oxfurd Street, but never saw no Oxfurd Universally there . . . jist departly mental stores. She got sum close fer herself at a big Teaton senter kinda plaice called Sellfishes, witch wuz so crowdid it seem like anuther zoo, and didn't live up to its name cuz they never sold any fishes. Terns out the naim of the store wuz Sellfridges, but Valeda sed they didden sell fridges neether, jist a lotta close. But the best thing happin to her in Lundun wuz finding a londrymat fer dubble dipping hers and mine undywares! This wuz after she had bot all them noo unmen-shunables in Sellfishes.

I had more luck wen I tuck a chants and plunched into yer Lundun Undyground and got took fer a ride. Wen I cum up fer ayr, first thing I seen wuz yer Lundun Britch, witch is a tawdler in age (one senchury) cumpair to ther Excommunication Tower itself (nine hundert yeer). Next thing I notice wuz a bit of the old Roaming wall put up centurions ago by yer Leegions. That's gotta be mebby 55 B.B.C. (Back Behind Christ) and, then I seen yer Water-gate (not the one that impared and unpeeched Richer Nickson but the wun put up about the yeer ten sexty sexish by Willyum the Conk Error). Then, by hinkus, I tern a round, and ther she wuz rite in frunta my ize! Yer Towering Lundun jist like on all the poached cards, with yer Beef Cakers in their beerds and bloomers hard by the drawbritches at yer Trader's Gait.

They don't like to be called Beefers . . . mebby sum of them is Vegetairy Aryans. All of them is Vet-Aryans of yer Army or yer Airfarce, but NOT yer Navey. That's cuz yeers ago them sailers wuz all press-ganged into serviss and never took a oaf to the Quean.*

Ther offishul titel is Yo-yoemen Wardens of yer Quean's Extra Ornery Gard. They bin doin this job fer nye on the nine hundert yeers, the oldest buncha men still carryin on the way they use to. They clame that they're the Queen's Boddy-gards but Her Majestick boddy don't cum near them so much enny more (mebby She nose sumthin I don't).

* FUTNOTE: Valeda always thot these fellas jobs wuz to tend the flours and insex on the grounds of pubic bildings, and that's why they were called Bee Feeders.

Lotsa famed and ill-famed peeple bin shut up in this horey old set of bildins incloodin' Quean Lizzybath hurself (yer furst, not yer secund). Wile still a teeny-aged printsess she wuz put in this Roil Hoosed-cow by her haff sister, Bluddy Merry. A cuppla the Vergin' Queen's lader boyfriends, yer Erls of Lester and S-sex, end up heer and had the blox put to them. Ann Bulloon wuz in fer a short time jist before she got the chop. Guy Focks wuz incarstrated heer after he tride to blow-up yer Parlmint bildins out of all pree-portions. During World war Eleven this bluddy Tower had a speshul visiter drop in, that beatle-browd Deppity Furor of Jermny hoo clamed he defe-cated frum Hittler's Nasty party, Rudolf the Red-face Hess.

Sir Water Rally, hoo invent cigareets, wuz in and outa this place, furst kept in by Quean Lizzybath and later by her suck-sesser Jaims Furst hoo hated terbacker, and ther's a sine in Rally's prizzun sell even today that sez "Nosmo King," but mebby that's the name of anuther prizzner.

I seen the Crown Joolhouse, but they don't give away any

*Towerin' sooveneer hunt*

soo Veneers. They got on dissplay a cuppla haff crowns, sum silver tunged strumpets, jooled sords, goaled flaggins, and lotsa maces (meece?), a wine cooler the size of a bathtub, and a reel sitdown tub fer them as gits the Order to take a Bath. They even got the Quean's Carnation roabs jist waitin fer Prints Charles if he ever gits round to it.

Wen I cum outside agin I seen hard by the Tower Britch, the Union Jacked up high on a big poll, and wuz pleeze to reed that it wuz a Dugless fur pervided by one of them Mick Millin Blowdells. It wuz a hunnert and atey five foot long, but the Birdish cut us down to size tryna git it acrost the Tems, cuz it wuz too big fer ther Bridges by a hundert foot.

The grounds wuz sure crowded that day, moseley skoolkids and Yanks and Japanknees flashers, but histerically yer Tower has allways bin a kind of a zoo. Gifts of aminals by forn poten-tapes started in 1235 with three leppers, sorry . . . lepperds, give to King Hennery the Three frum the Impurer Fredrick the Tooth of yer Holey Roller Umpire. Then cum a wite bare that use to fish in the Tems outside yer Tower; then Looey of Fran's sent a elfunt! That sure change the Housed Keeping rools, (a bigger shuvvel I bet) speshully wen it wuz follied by lyons and tygers, bares and apes, and even laffin hy-eenuses! It got so the beests wuz pushin the peeple outa the place, so about a sexy-sintenniel ago (150 yeers) they tuck them all over to Reejensee Park and started up yer Lundun Zoo ware Valeda watched all that munky bizness after she wocked out on yer Two Sods. She sed them English Prime mates got no manors atall but they keeps yuh laffin fit to bust. (She don't mean yer Cant Bishup of Archbury.)

All the aminals that's left in yer Towers now is jist yer Big Bird, hoo are consider by peeple heer to be Rave-in. Look to me like overstuff croze. They bin ther sints Henry Ate, (the wun with the sex wives) and they still keep at leest sex ravin on the grounds, with anuther yung cupple in the bullpit warmin up.

Them birds gits a speshul fud allowance frum the Birdish guvmint. They use to git their pick at the prizners hangin frum ther giblets. Nowadaze they git frut, aigs, the odd rabbit hed, and they'll even try ther beeks on tooryist's fingers holdin sangridges.

The roomer is that if them big black birds ever leevs that Tower then forn evaders will conker Britten. But this alreddy happens every summer. I have met them evaders, and they is us . . . overseize tooryists.

# Amster's Dam

THE HOOK ERS OF HAW LAND

HARLEM?

ROTTERS DAM

DOITS LAND

BULGIN AN TWERP

no.1 marihuana cannabis    sativa indica

# Amster's Dam

After Lundin we hedded strait fer yer Amster's Dam. All the way over on the Fairy Valeda was tellin me about yer Neverlands. She wuz like a liddle kid at Chrissmuss she wuz so eggcited. All her life, ever sints she red "Hams Brimker and his Silver Bobs" she has dreemed about skatin' in wooden shews past them winmills up yer alimentary canals beside yer Cider Sea wile the two-lips wuz in bloom. She sed them Dutchys is the cleenest peeple on erth. She don't have to tell me. I deels with sum of them vegible groars at yer Haul-in Marsh haffways down to Trauma, and you never met sitch a spick-spam bunch.

Valeda also wax leericle about the lokel Amsterdam painters. She didn't mean house or barnslappers, but them poortrait painters as duz peeple in oil fer a livin. Her faverit of yer Old Dutchmasters is Ram Bran. She figgers he musta had a day job cuz mosta his paintins isn't too well lit, like he wuz painting his subjex sumtime after choretime and supper. But he wuz a ringtale snorter of a dobber, wuz yer Ram Bran. Valeda swares they look so reel yuh cood take sum of his stuff fer folygrafts in a darkroom, and his retchings is pritty dark too.

The tuther artist Valeda fantsees, Vints Van Go, is anuther barl of fish. He's more of a landescaper, but he dun a few peeple like his docter and his postmen and hisself. Them Dutch pernounce his naim differnt . . . Vints Van Hock, or even van Gawk. Seems to be hard to pin him down cuz he wuz a bit of a Impressyunist. I ast Valeda if he dun as menny of them as our Ritch Liddle, but she sez Vince dint make that kinda Impression. Van Gock is doin' much better in the paint bizness now than wen he wuz alive. In fack, he oney got rid one of his Impressions the hole of his life. I gess Van Hock deescribes him best. Too bad he dint have a day job like Ram Bran.

It wuz Van Hock's last pitcher, a buncha crows in a corn-field, that turn him into a depressionist. Valeda sez yuh kin see the crow's feet in his sulfa-poortrait. I tole the wife that all them crows in our corn drives me crazy too. But accorn to his oney frend, Poll Go-agin, the bear-naked painter of Soused Specific ladees, Vints wuz a maniac-depressiv hoo used to tock his eer off about how he'd be better off if he'd of go with Go-gin fer the ile of Fidgity in yer South Seized.

Valeda wuz sure ther'd be a cuppla Exhibitionists showin off the both of them lokel artisticks in ther own hometown. But it wuz pritty dork wen we got to our hoetell, so we figgerd we better see the uther sites first. The sine on the bildin sed "Hoetell Grand . . . Crass . . . No Polskis." I thot at first it wuz rachel disincrimination till we found out it wuz jist the name of the Pole owned it. Valeda wonderd wat the Grand part wuz, but I tole her lader wen I got the bill that yer Grand wuz how much they charged us a nite.

It wuz a Sundy nite but Valeda hoped ther'd be one of them Inconveenients stores open so's she cood lode up on supplys so we wooden have to eet out. Soon as we got our new Selfridges close well hung, we wuz outside the hotell agin, on yer Grandam square. Lotsa sines in English all over the place so I figgerd them Dutchmen must be jist like mosta us Ontario-aryans, Ornjmen.

That big Damsquare musta bin a smoke-in airya, cuz it wuz fulla yung peeple all breethin' hard on the ends of cigareets with a funny kinda sickysweet smell. I ast one yung long-hare wat he was smokin and he sed it wuz grass seed. I didden say nuthin' to Valeda but I suspeck it wuz that Maxycan laffin ter-bacco they call the Maruh-jewa-hyena. I'd snift it before on our boy Orville wen he cum back frum one of them rotten roll con-sorts. Terns out it's purfickly leagle fer Amsterdamners to smoke the stuff and rite out in yer pubic squares too, without gittin in Dutch. Fer a minit I thot we wuz in a time-worp back in yer Swing-in Sextys amung sum flour childern hoo had gone to seed.

Down the street we found more than yer inconveenience store; it wuz a soopermarkit! The blinkin knee-on sine sed PORNO SUPERMARKET. We figgerd that must be the name of the prop rioter, like Fred Porno, and the S. and M. sine in the winder musta ment that he give out green stamps. Wat a shock

Amsterdam gits in Dutch with Valeda

we wuz in fer!!! It looked at furst a bit like a toystore, but it'd be hard to conseeve playin' with sich things. Instedda the kind of conveeniences we wuz lookin fer, ther wuz a deflate-a-bull vybratin' teen age doll that garnteed instint cumpanyunship, and a buncha fancy ticklers that wuzn't ment fer no armed pits.

Valeda thot she'd finely found the food sexion wen she cum upon picklin supplies under the sine that sed "DILL DOSE," but I steered her away quick over tord yer maggotzeens hopin' she cood git herself a *Shat Elaine* or a *Wimmin's Home Cumpanyun*. That wuz a big missteak. First one she pick up look like a derry report but insted wuz about a fella havin' animal husbandry with a cow. I don't think the wife reelized wat he wuz into, so I got her outa there, but not before she bot a postcard of Vints Van Gogo waring sunglasses. She cooden figger how he cood keep the blaim things on with one eer off.

Amster's Dam is offen called the Venus of the North on accounta its riddle with canals. Outside Mr. Porno's store ther wuz a little humpy bridge over one of them. And all along the sides of this hear canal wuz lotsa cullerd lites, mostly red.

We went past one of them redlites and ther wuz a woeman in a winda waving at us. Valeda wunderd if sum reel estait cumpny wuz havin open house. That wuz jist the big inning. Every winder on that longstreet had a redlite and a wavin' woman in it. I'd herd of yer Hook of Hawlin, but I dint reel-ize they wuz all stacked in one corner. Croozin them canals on fut wuz like goin up and down the iles of a Safeway Meetmarkit, only the meet wuz all standin up or sittin'down live on the hoof.

They say every town has its bizzy boddys but this carnyvo-ral display wuz outer control. Frum teenyagers to granmaws these wimmen wuz all on sail by the pound, and the more we seen of this meetmarkit the more deprest it (and us) looked. Valeda tuck a pitcher of me astin' one of them joy-girls (frum the French "feels de jaw") wat the charge wuz. It cost me 100 gilters ($75 US) wile Valeda flashed on her. Then I tuck a

How mutch is them pets in the winder?

pitcher of the wife full frontal outside one of them fornagraftic moovy stalls, jist in case the Ladees Aids back in Parry Sound didden bleeve wat we tole them we seen . . . Hamsterdam were nuthin' but a modren day Sod'em T'morra! Worsen that, Valeda pert neer had apple-plexy wen she seen that "F" wurd blinkin in lites advertizin' fore peeple co-opulating in a live-sex show! Ther wuz a yung fella out frunt wavin' us on in. At first he spoke at us in yer Doitch, cuz he thot frum the way we wuz drest that we cum frum Eest Jermny. But then he laps into Anglican Saxon. "Enuff window shoppin' fer now!" he sed, "Git reddy fer a brannew culcherl expeerients."

Before Valeda cood hit him with her hambag I wip her round the corner and in frunt of a place called "Durty Nelly's." Valeeda wanted to ball the heck outa me rite then and there, til I showed her the sine below "Durty Nelly's" sed "Ire-ish Pub." (I minded we had herda one with the saim naim back in Cork.) Sints ther wernt no wickit woman wavin' in the winder, and Valeeda wuz gittin' peckerish hongry, she cum in with me, speshully wen she seen a cuppla Salivation Army ladees cum-min out with take-out tees in ther mitts.

Terns out the pubican wuz reely frum Cork and tot foke dancin' to the dutchy lo-kels. Valeda wuz still a bit suspishus about F-words like foke, speshully the way he pernounced it, but she cam down after a plait of Irish stoo. He also had a ket-tle to make water and a pot to tee in, so I drunk the lot, wile Valeda had a Nire-ish cawfy and wernt long before she wuz singing along with them Poags on the pub's pubic address sis-tern.

Nex mornin we left Amsters Dam, and the rest of yer Neverneverlands, ferever I spose. Valeda wuz all dizzillusion about the decca-dance we had seen.

Bean simble minded she now susspected everything about the place as havin' sumthin' to do with sex, speshully the big colyum in the square acrost frum our hotel. To her it was nuthin' but a follicle simble to give Hamsterdammed men asspirations. To me, it sent a messedge of hoomility. She sed that wat this sin sitty needed was a good scrapin' of Old Dutch Klenser.

I ast her if she wanted to go to the country next door, Bellygum, and its Bulgin sitty of An Twerp. She sed "Nuthin' doin! If these Dutchburgers thinks we looks like Jermins then let's go there and mebby we'll feel to home!" Beesides, our busstour wuz heddin Jermany-ways and it mite be time to git a chants to git ourselfs back into our reserve seets.

Valeeda never did git to see the two-lips alongsider yer Cider Zee and the only winmills she saw wuz sum slut masheens in the trane station. But the wife still has her child-ish mammarys of wat the plaice shooda been, and first thing she dun wen we got on the Frankfurter trane wuz to reed me the old Dutch story about the liddle boy who saved the hole of his country by keepin his finger in a Dyke.

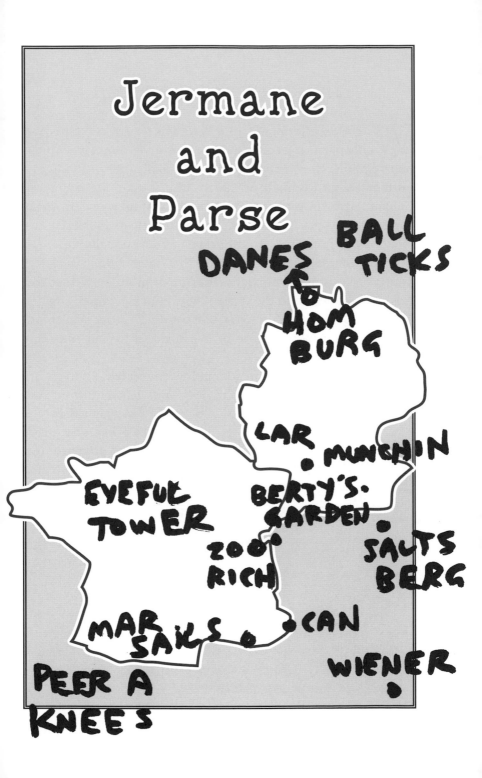

# Strickin Yer Doitch

We got on a Jermane trane hedding fer Lar, witch is the only place in Jermny that we noe on accounta we wunce had relations ther, Privet Redge Rumball, (the wife's granmuther wuz a Rumball on her muther's side) servicing yer Canajun Army in yer Seegrim Hylanders. Mind yew, our Armd Farces is no longer rezzident up to Lar now thanx to deesishuns maid by our preeviuss Encumbrance of a Nationally Offensiv Minster, Marsell My-Ass. Seams that they didden feel the kneed to keep us on our Nay Toes enny more, now that the Coal Wore is over, and the wirld is startin to blow up in smaller bits. But all this is makin extry work fer yer Untied Nayshins, witch meens Canda is more in the thicks of it than ever, but with no basis in Yerp.

The wife luv that trane so much we deesided not to git off it at Lar or even Badmen Solingerin sints hardly nun of our boys wuz at eether spot. We wud hav luv to stop off in yer Black Forst fur a peesa cake, to go with the mane food on that trane witch wuz the wurst. I don't meen it wuz bad. The wurst over heer is reely hot dawgs, eggsept ther bettern the weenys

Lunchin in Munchin

we gits back home. If yer confuze it's becuz of the Jerman lan-gridge. "Wurst" is Doitch fer hot-dog, and it wuz serv by a wader hoo clame he wuz a Frankenfurter and his muther wuz a Hamburger. I figgerd he wuz havin us furners on, altho' the Jermins is quite carnal-omniveruss about meet eetin. Bad don't meen to Jermins wat it meens to us. "Bad" is sumthin you do on a Sardy nite. You take that place Bad'un-Bad'un ware we stop off fer a cuppla hours. It jist meens havin' a bath twice, witch is wat we dun along with hunnerds of uther peeple kickin up ther heals in a big hot pool and a friggid one after.

Valeda had got herself a Anglish-Jermin dickshunairy but she wuz too bizzy rubberneckin' cuz the trane follied yer Rime river, and the wife started Cassel-watchin on yer Rind, so I started lookin' up Jermin wurds so's I cud becum bi-lingamal. I didden lern much but it wuz furst-rate enertainmint.

It wuz a eddication to reed wat uther peeple calls things. A cassel wuz yer shlosh, a catheedrill is a Dum, a savins bank is yer Spark Ass, a taxi is a Mietwagen, a ellyvater boy is a Fahrtstuhlfuhrer, a Joolry store is Uren and jooolry itself is Shmuck.

Them Jermins got more cassles per square hed than the resta the wirld put together. I red about wun bilt by a crazy king, Ludd Wig of Bovaria (the only nutty sun of the Impurer Max A Million). His dreem cassle wuz oney bilt farely reesent during Senchury 19. In fack it looks jist like the mickymouse set-up they got at Dizzlyland. That dun it. The wife wanted to see it. That ment we got off the trane before Bertie's Garden, the Nazty luv nest ware Adolf Hittler admired Eva's Brawn on top of ther mounting.

That farey tail lookin cassle became to be cald called Slosh Noise Swans Teens. To git ther we hadda rent anuther car after lunchin in Munchin, witch is wat the lokel Mewnickers calls ther sitty, and on the way to that Dizzy lookin cassle we got cot in a Shtow, witch is Jermin fer traffical jam. Tuck us three ours

At the
rong
Dizzlyland

moovin ded slow in a bumper to bumper crop of tooryists, not
wun of witch wuz our lost buss. Valeda felt like we wuz back
in Nooyork, cuz we wuz on the rite side of the rode agin, but
stuck with no change of seenery.

That cassle wuz a offal dissapointment. Not as a bildin
mind . . . but ther wuz no whoop yer loops or enny uther kinda
kiddy rides like they has at Canda's Blunderland or even yer
Canajun Nashnul Exibitionists. There's no detractions fer
tooryists atall on the land round them fancy piles. No wunder
I red after we got hoam that this Yerpeen Dizznyland wuz
havin its fine-anchull whoas.

# Whizzing to Oz

In all our haist we never thot to check on that rumaway buss
with our luggridge. After Lundin I thot Valeda wood be too
nerviss to try a forn fone but she took the Bell by the horns,
tride a 1-800 nummer, and by swinjer she found out our blong-

ings wuz hedded fer Saltsberg over the boarders into Oztria. Eether we kep up the chase in a sirius way or we start buyin local geer. That ment a drive thru the mountings of yer Oztrian Tee Roll. Valeda wuz not too keen on that till I tole her it wuz the saim mountings ware they film her faverit moovy "Yer Sound of Mewsick." She hum the hole thing all the way wile I accompany her by blowin my nose, to the sound of mucus.

I dunno how that July Androos ever got herd by the cammeras wen she sung that song on the toppa that mounting, cuz them hills is alive with cows and they all got bells on, and the jingle jangle is interminabull, not to menshun yer cowpies. Valeda sed that moovy makes Oztria look like the nicest place in the wrild, but bleeve me with them cows, ya gotta watch yer step.

We staid at a Inn that musta bin run by Cappin von Trapp's cussin, Toorist von Trapp. We hardly got a winka sleep on accounta his dam dogs never shut up all nite. Them Bavarian bitches wuz yowlin under our windas till the sills were alive with the hounds of Mewnick!

Deer lad:

Thinkin of you wen we visit the berthplace of Moss Hart. He writ his first sympathy before he wuz five yeer old, and wuz makin a good livin fer his famly by twelve. X marks the room ware he dun all this. Have you cleened yers up lately? And the barn?

Yer luvving pairnts.

Saltsberg is a nice refine town, noan mostly fer bein the berth-place of that Wolf Gang MossHart, (he writ "I'm Inclina Knock musick") and ther's a Festeral in his Honner. But the tooryist buss lady sed that the Sounda Muzak toor out-drawers Moss Hart's hy mucky muck Festeral by ten to wun. Every bloo-hared femail tooryist wants to git a helluvacopper ride to the film's ackshell low-cajuns as they sing "I am sixty, goin on seventy."

We found out we mist our bus agin. That driver musta bin taking time off frum yer Injun-Anal-Apples 500! We ast about the ware-abouts of a tooryist buss outa Lundin by way of Hamstersdam that we had bin trine to foller, but the Frow bee-hind the Sue-veneer counter sed they had cum offa their buss, bot post carts, and then every-buddy got back in it fur to con-tinyew to Wean. This confuze Valeda and me, speshully sints ther wuz a cuppla nuns on that buss, not to menshun sevral mails. Turns out that Wean is wat they call yer capitol of Oztria, Vee-enema, and the capitolists therselfs are all Weaners.

Back in the rent-a-car, and more cows, more bells, and more harepin terns than I cood shake the stick at. The wife is alla bubble about goin all that way to the home of Joe Ham Strouse, the Walts King.

We wuz suprize wen we got there to find the hole town shut down tite . . . and on a Thirsdy affernoon! Nuthin seem to be open. The tooryist buss place that mite of had our lug-gridge wuz snapshut. Not having a interdpritter handy, I look up my Handy-speek book and ast wun of the lokel Frow Lines "Voss mocks?" (Wat in the samhill is not goin' on?) "Voe ist Yadermann?" (Where IS everybuddy?)

"Christie Himmelfart!" sez she.

"Charlie Farquharson!" I replys.

But terns out that this is a vurry Cathlick sitty and Christie Himmelfart meens Assension Day (wen HE went up to Hevven). Huttels wuz open tho', and ther wuz room at the Inn, so we book in nex door to Sittyhall (it's called yer Rathouse).

On the cawfy tabel ther's a hambook print up in Anglish, advertizin a Artsy Festeral goin on in town that Valeda sed wood make a combine of yer Strafford, yer Shah, and yer Parry Festeral of the Sound look down rite cheez-paring.

Valeda likes all this kinda hy mucky muck stuff even bettern Bingoe. This wuz a sex weak Culcher Festeral. The big tickit wuz fur Rich Waggoners "God-Damnerung" opry, witch they sed cum strait frum yer Babe Rooth Festeral!! (Valeda sed it wuz yer Bay Root Festeral, but isn't that ware yer Mid-least Lesbians lives?) Ennyways, it sounded like sex hours of hevvy mettle, so Valeda give it a pass.

Ther wuz more culcher loose in this place than a vat of pencilinen. Yer Volks Teeter (theater fer plane fokes) had more poplar stuff like "Dee Flittermouse" (The old Bat . . . Valeda took it kinda pursnal), and "Der FlySchitz" (untranslate-a-bull).

But that wuzn't on till the nex day wen this town wood became a open sitty agin. We seen that Grand Ole big Opry house. It wuz wun of them fancy twurly curly-cute pubic bildins that wuz put up durin' the sitty's Broke peeriod, so I spose with all that sudsidize culcher, they're still payin' them all off.

So wat did us Farquharsons end up doin' in all this corny-copious of culcher? Streetwockin, that's wat. They got free ennertanemint in the Veeknees streets without goin in no Opry House. There wuz a Indie-amneezian gurl playin' wat Valeda called a baby sitar, whangin away on it to her harp's contempt. Then we started

Havin' a blowout in Swishyland

watchin' sum street busters playin with therselfs in the middla the rode with bloograss and foke and uther middla the rode mewsick. They wuz usin a geetar, a mandlin and a warshtub with a screwdriver witch they use as a base fidel.

And they undressed the crowd in Anglish! Wun fella cum frum Tamper, Florider, anuther frum Hyfer, Izzreel, and last and mebby leest a umpteen-ager frum Rich Man's Hill, Ontaryo! We bot ther seedy tape so's they cud afford to have supper.

We deesided nex day to reely put on the feedbag. The lokels heer are big winers, but also creemers. I think Ween muss be the wipcreem capital of yer wirld. Them Weeners eether sits inside ther hoy riggers (wineshops) and becum regler winos all day, or sit outside on ther sidewocks and slirp up caffays mitt slag (pernounce slog) and eet a peesa choclit cake called a Sacker Tort that is richern Creases or even Comrad Black.

Weeners is big ice screemers too. Valeda and I sat in ein park and et a big sundy cuvverd in slag and lissen to Walt's musick, "Weenerblud" by her faverit, Joe Ham Strouse's, and Fran's Lay Har hoo had cremated yer "Murry Widda." We jist sat back and bob our heds in three quarters time, nockin back calorys and shakin the fat round our harts, and dam yer klessterall!

# Yer Swish and Yer Lick den Steins

Them cleen close and that tooryist buss that we had bin chasin' sints Barmy Cassel wuz somewares in Wee-enema, but I'll be danged if we cud find hidener hares of it. We finely give up, lingeryin' only long enuff to buy ourselfs sum more smalls. Our noo underlings wuz all ornj-cullerd like they wuz fulla vittamine C!

We hedded fer Swishyland. Them Swishes is try-lingamal, so we lernt to say "Gimmy the check" in three langridges ("Dee Zahlen Bitte!" "Eel condo, pray go," and "Laddition, silver plate.")

We et Swishy cheese on top of a mounting direck frum a cow with bells on, so that it didden hav time fer to git enny holes in it. Then it wuz back in the car with more harepin terms goin round them mountings. We outskirted all the big towns, Burn, Bazzle, Zoo Ritch and Gin Heaver. Ther wuz a lotta liddle rivers mebby six inches deep, like that sammon catchin place in Noo Brunsick, yer Mirror Mashee.

It's a shame them mountings has to be there, cuz they spoils the seenery. If it wernt fer them big snow-cuvverd humps Swishyland wood look as nice as yer Prints Edwards Eyeland. And if they prest all them mountings flat, I betcha this liddle country wood be jist as big as Canda.

william Tells Charlie to hold still

Nex to them Swishes, tween it and Fran's, is a little country no bigger n yer grounds of yer Canajun Nashnul Exhibitionists in Trawna. It's called Lickdensteen, but it shood reely be called Lickdenstamps, cuz that's ther number one hevvy industry.

Not too menny cars, but a lotta bysickles with peeple peddling therselfs. It's a peecefull plaice. We staid in a penshun (that's not wat yuh gits in yer oldage, it's wat yuh stays in wen yuh goes to Yerp in yer oldage.) Our penshun wuz nex door to a buncha cows in a feeld, and ther bells didden keep us awake, they lull us fass a sleep. We muss be gittin used to wat them Catlicks calls yer rithm methud.

Nex day wuz the mornin rush-hour, but more like Parrysound than Nooyork. All the cars goin by our penshun wuz hung up, behind them caddle mooving on to anuther pastyer. That's sitty life in Lickdensteen!

No londrymats neether. Before we noo it we wuz without a change a outer-close frum wat we wuz standin up in. (And they wuz startin to feel like they cood stand up fer themselves.) Valeda sed ther's oney wun place fer to shop fer close, speshully hats, (and mine she sed wuz a disgraze). We went to Zoo Ritch, handed in our rendercar and tuck the trane to Parse.

# Parse, Fran's

Ther wuz a few tooryists on the trane, but a lotta Frenchmin too, with boddles of whine and long loafs of bred lookd like fallicle simbles. I figgerd they wuz all goin to chirch cumunion but it tern out to be jist ther lunch. Smelt gud too. We never had a bad meel wen we wuz in Fran's.

By trane yer outer-skirts of Parse looks like enny uther urbane burg. It's oney wen ya gits deep inside and away frum yer slumberbs that it seems to spruice up. Mostly by not bein so blaim plastical modren. I tole Valeda, Parse is kinda like yew, its nicer the older it gits. She giv me the rong kinda a look.

On the train cummin in to yer Glare dullEst (Mid Eest trane station) Valeda kep tockin about goin to yer Loo. I sed they got wun at the end of the corrydoor, but ya better go now cuz they don't like it wile yer standin in the station. She sed she wuznt tockin about a Briddish-stile warshroom. Yer Loo wuz the place ware the painters wuz. I figgerd the seets wood be dry by now, but she wuz deefurring to sum kinda artsy galley that's run by a woeman call Moaner Leesa. The gidebook showed a pitcher of yer Venis de Meal-o, sumwat the wurse fer ware. On the postcart Valeda bot she look purfickly armless to me. (Veenis, not Valeda).

Even yer sitty Hall in Parse is a place ware yuh kin git put up fer the nite, on accounta its called yer Hoetell dee Vill. Our Parse hoetell had sumthing reely Counternentil . . . a B-Day . . . witch look to us like sum unfinnish plummin. I cooden figger wat the doosh it wuz, so I ast the conky-urge (rum clerk). Valeda thot it mite be fer to warsh a baby in. He snicker and sed no, it wuz fer to warsh the baby out.

We maid plans fer to see Paree and find out why after we seen it, like the old song sez, we cooden be kep down on the farm. Valeda still hoped that mebby we mite ketch up with our busstoor at Charters. Sounded loggicle to me, cuz most tooryist busses is charters, but terns out it's the name of a fame-uss middel-age church. The wun thing I wanted to see wuz yer Mule End Rooge, like I seen in the moovy of the saim naim with that liddle short painter, Too Loose Low Trick, brushin them boomps-yer daisy gurls that's kickin up ther heals and shakin ther can-cans. Then top it off with a vizit to yer Fall Ease Brazeers (ware they don't ware enny). I never got nowares neer them.

Parse is a sitty fulla britches under witch is a lotta liddle boats flyin by (Baddo mooches) in Sane. That river is the best way fer to see downtown Parse. Bettern yer slubway witch is run by yer Metro jist like Trawna. But them flyboats goze between yer Reeves Adroit and Goash (Banks on yer Rite and Banks on yer Left). So we dun it, and it's jist like yer steemer Seekwin in Parry Sound, sept that there's more to see on these leffin rite banks than effergreen trees and rox fulla preecrambian shist.

Eeziest thing to see frum pratickly anywares is the wirld's biggest Meckanno set, the Eyefull Tower, witch is kind of a X-raid vergin (jist the bones showin) of Tronto's CNN tower. The wife had all kinds of uther places on her mind, incloodin yer Loovers (the arty musuleum that I had confuse with the bathroom), yer Ark de Tree Umph, yer Garden Tooleries, the big cherch on a liddle eyeland that used to have yer haff back of Noted Daim wringin his bells. And speshully most of all fer Valeda, Moe Marter ware all them commershul artists livs wile dobbin and drinkin cocain.

They also have a Hoetell fer Invalides, and a Pally Roil, but we felt we had that'un cuvverd cuz they alreddy got wun of them in Tronto. (The wife and former sweetart and I bin ther wunce yeers ago to dants in fronta Burt Noisy's Orkester.) The big noo bilding that looks outa place in Parse, cuz it's so modren, is yer Sal Puppy Doo. Valeda sed she'd druther visit the Catty Combs (Pile a Bones) or yer Sorebone Universally (ware all the Quirepracticers granulates, I spose). Furst thing she dun tho' wuz go to a outside flee markup (Marsh o'Pukes) and git me a berry fur my hed so's I'd look more frenchyfide.

We had dinner (lunch) at a Beastroe on yer Shams Ellyzay. I had a Crock Ma Sewer (hot ham sanrich) and the wife a hareball amulet, and both wuz deelishus. We wuz in site of yer Ark de Tree Ump, and thru it ya kin see the noo Ark put up to celibate yer by-sextenniel of yer French Resolution. Our huttel wuz neer enuff by on yer Ruse Sin Honner eh? so we deeside to wock back thru yer Plotz della Conkerd. Valeda had once seen a noozreel about cars whippin round and round them Plotzes (Frenchy roundybouts) with no way out fer no pederastrians.

Well sir, Parse is a bewdyfull sitty, but ther's no gittin round it. Ther's more fast trafficking goin on than I ever seen enny place before. Don't ever try crossin that Ruse de Conkerd as a pederastrian. And it don't help fer to watch the siggonals. Them lites don't pertane to nothin' that I cood see. Valeda thinks they wuz jist a rews to git innersent toryists out in the middla all them veehicles reshin by, so's we'll git to patteronize wun of their hospiddles. They say sumbuddy is nock down in Parse traffick every fifteen minits of the day. I dunno how that poor person kin stand it.

We shet our eyes and sumhow maid it acrost. Alluva suddin we wuz in fronta yer Joody Pam. "Never mind that Moaner Laser!" sed Valeda, "This is ware all the frenched impreshunists hangs out: Manny, Moany, Day Gas, Piss Arrow, and a dotty painter call George Sewerat." I never herd of any of them, but we went in and I took one look at them watterd Lilys by that clod Moany, and they wuz so reel ya felt ya cood reech out, touch them, and wet yerself.

Safest and most expansiv way to git round Parse is to take tacksees. Speshully on speshul acadians like Valeda's berfdy. Don't madder if yuh cant speek the garlic, cuz them drivers got more jestyers than yule ever need in Shrades. Our driver had his liddle dog in the frunt seet beside him, and the dog talked more than the driver ever did.

Nex we hed fer yer big lammark, yer Eyefull tower where I pose in fronta Valeda's Browny with my new Frenched berry and a liddle mustash I maid frum her macnamara fer yer eyes. I pertended like I wus not a tooryist but a lokel yokel, and then fer a berfdy sprize I tuck her back ther at nite to go to yer Jools Ferns Restrunt. It sounded like it'd be twenny thousand leeg under see, but it wer rite at the top of that Tower.

And watta meel we had up yer Eyefull! It started out with petty

Gettin' the pointa being in Parse

pains (not akes and gripes, but liddle hot breds). Valeda got crabs with her soo flay, and I hadda pidgin sallid . . . the saim birds as wuz sittin on the rale of the tower watchin me as I et ther rellativs!! It looks like purply beef and taist kinda like chickens livvers, but bedder. Mane corse wuz lam with artsy chokes.

They brung her speshul berfdy deesert with a candel stickin out of a choclit doam that wuz cuvver with ammonds and cumsquats. And the intire meel wuz liquid-dated by a bottla sham pain, witch reely stird up the Homogoblins in my bludstreem! Then they give eech of us truffels to top it all . . . they're sposed to be extry speshul pig food, but it seams too good fer them nosy porkers.

Bean her navel day, Valeda wuz determine to git in her dose a culcher, utherwise she wood feel as rangy as a cut cat. So she chose the opry "Aida" (pernounced "I, Eater," witch seemed approapriat to me after the meel we jist had). Valeda had seen it afore at yer Royl Alecs theeyater with the Sand Carload Opry. It musta bin a resessionary vergin with lots of cutbacks cuz they dun yer big Try-Umphrey Prade with oney 1 trumpit, 1 thrombone, 2 simbles and 7 soljers, so that they kep runnin rond the back and cumming back on stage pertending to be sumbuddy elts.

Valeda had mist the big "I Eater" show at yer Skydoom with ellfunts witch had left a grate depressyun on everybuddy, (speshully the maintnunts staff after a cuppla the packy-dermis left sooveneeers on stage the size of a Folksywagon). So she wanted to be sure and ketch this Parse hy-mucky-muck show witch wuz run off not at yer Opry House but in a indore sports stayjim biggern yer Make Beleef Gardings.

The story in I-Eater is about a buncha Frenchmen singin Eyetalian in Eejippt. It wuz like a combynation of yer Sope opry on the TV and the Sandy Claws prade. It had haff the Frenched army in it as extrys and a gurls quire frum Veroney, ware Romeo and Joolyit use to live till they dyed. The upshat of the hole evenin wuz that Valeda shure looked liked the cleen look of Eejippt, and fer our weddin analversry she wants to go ther. But only if we gits on a busstoor cuz we don't speek enny Eyetalian and only "un pew" French, and nun atall of yer Jippsy. Nex day we got our conchy urge to fone up the busstoor peeple, and it seams that our strangers (and I hope our close) wuz gittin off the buss and takin a trane fer Venus! That didden make sents to me, cuz you'd have to be asternuts fer to even think of goin there. But Valeda sez it's Vennis, not Veenis, and the reezon busses can't go there is it's all under water. So I sed why shood we go ware the fluds are and git our feet wet? We'll git stuck fillin sandbags fer them dykes. But Valeda sed it's bin under water fer hunderds of yeers and they's nuthin' they kin do about it now.

# Expresso
# to Venus

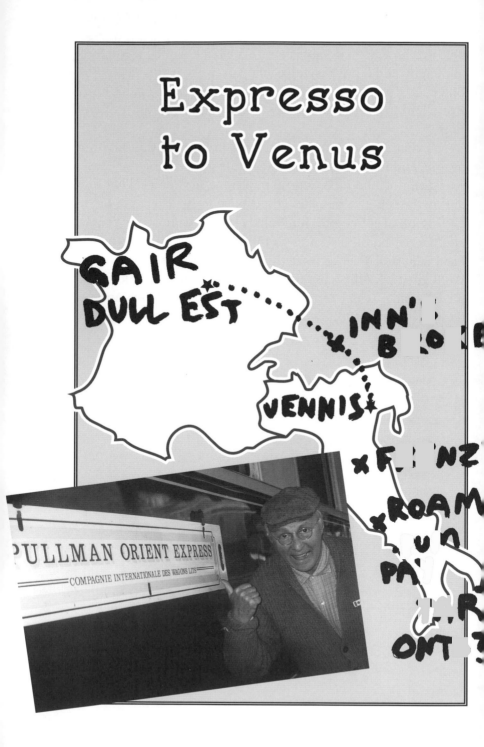

# Yer Rale on Agin

The oney trane goin to Vennis rite away wuz yer Orry Entrail Express. I'm not too keen on that Chinee fud, but Valedee luvs all that slubgum and dim sons. And we hadda ketch up with our luggridge cuz my Polly Esther swetter wuz gittin longern longer with all that warshing. It's maid of simpathetick mateerials and its garnteed not to shrink, but it shure ain't garnteed not to keep goin tords my kneeze till it looks like a wullen dress! So we manedge to git reserved on that Oreeintail Expresso the wife and I.

It's a purty slick lookin train, all politched wud and shiney brass. Makes yer VIA rails back home feel like frate. Alluva sudden it hit Valeda, that this wuz the saim train she had seen in a moovy about peeple gittin' merdered in ther births. I hate to giv it away, but I red that book on the trane, and it maid me shiver in my shift cuz ther wuz eleven suspecks and ever one of them dun it! It wuz a Hollow Wood moovy ten yeers ago that brung this trane back frum oblivia. But it don't go on past Vennizz to Buddy Pest and I Stand Bull like it use to.

Wen we went to dinner, it looked like all the waders wuz sittin down on the job, but terns out they wuz cussdummers drest like waders, black boa tyes and tuckseedoes. Ther wimmen wuz gussied up too, all dun up like pink pigs at markit timc as my old Dad uscd to say. Wun of them wuz all undressed up in wat Valeda calls a gownless evening strap, with a fur, stole. (Frum ware she nicked it, I cooden say.)

Beside the plaits ther wuz all kindsa eaton tools. Morn wun of eech of yer nives and forks, but Valeda sez ya has to go frum the outside in, jist the same way the fud goes down yer hatch. I got morn a bit confuze and end up stern my tee with a fishfork.

The scoff in yer Dine-in car wuz pritty fantsy. They start out with paddy foe grass, witch is reely gooses slivers all smashed up. Then munkfish, witch taist like a mixed marge of a lobster maited with a veel. I thot we wuz finnish wen they give us a Sore Bay (French fer a Surebet). But it wuzzen deesert, it wuz jist fer to fresh up yer pallet fer the mane corse witch wuz a meet pie call Beef Well-In-Tun with scalped potaters and charred Swish.

Fer our deserts we had wat look like hard hats . . . not the sent candy we use to buy as kids along with our Bolo Bats . . . but a brown doam, and inside wuz toffy all gingerd up, with three razzburys on the side in a yella sweet soss. It wuz a rang-dang-doo of a meel and Valeda will sure have to hussle fer to pleaze me like that.

After dinner we wuz invite to repare to the lieberry car fer brandy and snaps. Valeda is teetote-all so she spent all her time in the liddle buttock, (she sez it's call a boo-teak) buying up anything witch sed Orientail Express on it. She clames she dun all her Chrismuss shoppin sex munths erly. I declare I dunno wat she's gonna say to our Customs after they looks twice at her wen we gits back hoam.

But we coodna bin serviced better than we wuz on that trane. At nite they pull down and pull out things so that we wuz deliverd of seprit births, Valeda on her lowers and me on my uppers. That's on accounta the wife cant stand no hites. She got regler vertigro cumming thru yer Madderhorns. I think she saw mosta Swishyland with her eyes close. That nite

Valeda slept like a lawg, but I staid up in my uppity bunk reedin that merder book about yer Expresstrane that maid me sus-pishus of all them peeple we et dinner with.

Breckfust wuz serve in our liddle cumpartmint, countinental stile witch meens no porritch or uther seerials, but a lotta crotch ants (French crullers) with jamson jellys. Gittin off the trane wuz yer hard part. Valeda she wanted to stay on ferever and git waded on hand and fut. And she tip everybuddy like she wuz payin ther yeerly rents. But I agrees with her about gittin serviced like that. It's gonna be hard to git use to yer Veeya Rails agin ware there's not even a conduckter on bored fer to take yer tickit, but they send sum kid up frum the baggidge car fer to stamp on yer forehed "THIS SIDE UP."

# Water Town

The wiles Valeda wuz sinkin in the lucksury on that Orientailed Exprcss I wuz lookin out the window and checkin on yer Eyetalian veggy-tation. The rodeside had lodes of wiled poppys and spy-orrhea, and ther wuz feelds of cultyvated poppys too. I wonderd if they wuz harvested to make opee-yum fer them dopey ad-dicks. Ther wuz lotsa vimyards stuck up by Poles fer winos, Yerp's most poplar drink.

I mind Valeda had tocked about how romantickal it wuz all gonna be, lookin at palisses and cherches. Well sir, wat I wuz seein as we got close to Venus wuz hardly all that. All I seen wuz a smokestacked jungel of hevvy indestry with peterochemmycull plants poring fourth clowds of yella gas. The oney refined thing about the place seam to be them big oil tanks everywares.

Valeda wuz tocking to the trane stoord about the best artsy galleys fer to go to see, so I ast him about all the industererial pollyution I had jist bin lookin at. He put his noze in the air and sed that that wuzn't Vennis, but a place called Mestry ware mosta the Veneezians lives, and commutes to ther tooryist jobs every day.

By swinjer, he wuz rite. Cuz after we got off the trane, and trundel our luggridge to the water, it wuz heddin on fer sunset, and wat I seen before my eyes beets even the pitcher of Vennis I seen on that hardwear calender in the Eyetalian barbershop in Parry Sound. Everything wuz pink and ornj and pail purpel, and all the bildins wuz in what Valeda calls yer sillowet. I agreed with the wife that wut wuz all wet about Venniss wuz me. Valeda wonderd why all them Venusians peeferred to live in that smokestacked slum Mestry insted of in this palacial Dizzyland, but that's wat happens with tooryism. The pezzants and pee-ons have to moove out to make way fer the likes of us. Happens back home in Muskoker too.

Ther wuz lodes of tooryists wading on the doc fer a bote fer to take them over to this Pairadice. Valeda thot we'd be druv acrost in a gondole, but insted they had fairy botes with inbred motors called vapid-rettos. And mirrorkill of mirrorkills, wile we wuz lined up fer to git on one of them things, Valeda reckanize a buncha fellow-waders as the voyeurs on that Ire-ish buss at Blarmy Cassel!

After all our drivin round hare-pins terns, and catchin' tranes and faerys, heer they all wer jist standin still lookin at us as if we wuz a site fer sore eers. I didnt mind any of them frum before, but they all minded us rite away. Mostly becuz ther bustdriver had bin minding our luggridge all the way frum Ire-land and it kep gittin in the way of everybuddy eltses.

Valeda wuz so releef cuz now she cood ware her old close, and folly the resta the pack all thru all them galleys and chirches and she wood heer it all in her own langridge. I wuz even more releefed becuz it ment a fresh change of longjons.

They all went off to ther huttel, yer Gritty Paliss, witch didden sound too cleen to me, but Valeda sed it got forestars in the revues. We cooden sine up at the saim hoetell as our fella busstooryists, becuz ther wuz no room at ther inn. I maid a joke about gittin' a single with a stall in the stabel jist like yer Holey Famly but nobuddy laffed, espeshully knot Valeda. So we hadda plump fer a extry expansiv dump hard by yer Grand canal, witch is alimentary to this town cuz if it wuz a street it'd be yer mane street. Bleeve me I cood git use to a town that had no trafficking with oddy-mobeels.

Valeda and me stroll about with our fella tooryists lookin fer a place to put on the feedbag, and it sure is nice not to worry about cars gittin' ya rundown. The mane mennis in Vennis is gittin' side-swipe by a backpacker lookin fer a Yooth Hostile before it closes. Wat elts ya has to git use to is clime-in over all them britches. Seams to me yer up and over wun of them stoned things every ten secunds.

I wisht we had staid with that steemed fairy we cum over on. It stops all over the iles jist like a watery streetcar, and that gives ya yer best ideer of the hole town as its laid out. They's a lotta soo-idge up yer canals but it gits flush out twice a day with yer Tide. Under pert neer every wun of them britches we crossover was passing a gon-dull-ear fulla tooryists. Valeda wuz disap-point that the oresman wuzn't singin "O Solar Meow" wile he worked. I jist kept starin' at his gondoler and wondrin' how in the sam hill Foster Huey way up hy in yer Make Beleeve Gardings cood have ever brodcast a hole hocky game in wun of them tipsy things.

Gone
Dull
Ears

We end up out on the street havin our supper in a canal-side restrunt witch maid it handy fer to hock and spit. The menyou cum in English asswell as Veneeshun. Valeda orderd cuddlefish cuz she thot it sounded kinda cute. I orderd Livver witch they dun it up ther own Venusian way, and it coz me to brake wind in unexpectorated places fer the nex three days. Valeda's fish cum all cuvverd in ink, and she tride to send it back, but her fella tooryists tole her that a cuttlefish is a kind of ocktoepuss, and the soss wat looks like Injure ink is jist its sulfa-deefents aginst uther pre-daters. Valeda hates them ate-armed things ever sints she seen Kirt Dugless rassle with wun of them big suckers twenny thousand leegs under the see, so she hardly tutched her meel, wile I et that liver fartoo much.

Our huttel on the Gram Canal wuz two palisses put together and called Yeroper and Regina. It sounded to me like a combynation of inns in Bellyfast and Sassacatchewin, but it didden tern out to be a dump atall, probly the nicest nite's lodgin we had bin in, next to yer Ire-ish Longvillains. Mind jew, we didden sleep too good, not on accounta the bed, but the bells. And not the bells in yer hoetells or swingin with them Swish cows. Them blaim chirches heer lets off their peelers every our, and on the haff our too. Valeda thinks it's calling peeple to Vespers, but I tole her them Eyetalian moter scooters wuzn't aloud in this place.

I decided I wuzn't too sure I wuz all in faver of the wife and me rejining our tooryist party. It felt more cumferbull gittin back into my old duds and it were nice to think of leevin the drivin to sumwun elts, but I don't like bein led around by the nose fer to waller in the troff of culcher. I cooda cheerfly staid home in that hoetel and looked out on yer elmentary canal life, like wen I sit on my vranda and watch the summer traffick on the rode to McKellar. Insted we lined up with our fella tooryists, and follied sum lady with a umbreller like she wuz the Pie-eyed Piker of Hamilton.

But Valeda wuz determin to cum back frum Yerp all culchurd. So nex day we lined up like Chillderns Day at yer Canajun Nashnul Exhibitionists, and follied this gide uppendown britches and in and outa all them chirches lookin at the saim blaim things in every wun. It's my pinion that wen ya've seen wun Eyetalian cherch, ya've seen them all. God nose I got nuthin agin yer Vergin' Merry and her little Holey boy, but I got offal tired of lookin' at all them pitchers of the two of them, speshully wen sumtimes the babey looked fer all the wirld eether like that moovy acter Rod Stiger, or Micky Ruiny (and I meen the older vergin). Valeda wuz startin to look pritty poopt frum all this hevvy upliftin'.

Evrybuddy flocks ta Vennis

I liked it better wen I staid outside in Sinmark's Square wile the rest of them drooped into that big cherch of the saim name. Frum the outside that holey bildin looks Roosian Orfadocks with its union bulbs like they has in Mawscow's Crumlin hard by yer Red squairs. (Ackshully this chirch is not desined so much Serviet Unyun as wat they call yer Bizzyteens.) Best thing about it is way hy up on the front there's four prantsing stedes. I thot they wuz yer Forehorses of yer

Apocketclips . . . but them nags terns out to have blonged to yer Impurer Neero, the fella that fiddled with hisself wile the resta Roam got berned.

Wile Valeda and the bunch wuz trapesin' thru this old cherch bildin, I stuck with the resta the marks and squares on Sin Marks squares. I bot sum seedcorn and a Gon-dull-ear hat and had my pitcher took as a pirch fer them pidgins. I had a lotta fun actin' as a scaired-crow fer them plump fetherd fiends, and I kep thinkin of the gratemeel I had at yer Eyefull Tower on wun of them things. I wuz temted to grab wun wile it wuz eeton outa my hand and wring his neck fer dinner, but I didden think the cheef sheff in our hoetell wood depreciate it, and ther wuz no kitchin up in our rumes. They say ther's a pidgin fer every square hed in this town.

It seems to me that Vennis is the only burg I cum across that has got more tooryists than rezzddents, and accorn to the sadisticks I am rite. Every day a hunnert thousand furrin outlanders pores in to this place, wile the rezzddents yeer after yeer pores out, permamintly. Sum to sluburbs like Mestry and uthers to more fern parts, till this town nowadaze has got a lot lesson a hundert thousand sittyzens. Most of them as fleas the sitty is yung, and Venniss has end up as a retiredmint villedge fludded sex months of the yeer by transee-unts like us. In the winter it's more deeserted than Florider in the summertime, and I offen wunderd how them runty liddle cats that runs around everywares manged to git ther winter feed.

This has been a tooryist town pritty much sints before yer Middel-ages wen that Ire-ishman Mark O'Polo brung spigetty back frum Chiner, and they found their fewcher was in their pasta. Ther's a lotta roomers that Venniss shood pass a movement on the floor of its town hall (the Dog's Paliss is wat it's called) stating that tooryists is the limit, cuz they have reeched it. Them Venusians is wurried that all them trompin feats is gonna shake down their sitty sumday. Sum lokels feels all us forn inturd-lopers shood hav to hav a Visa before we cums in.

(That'd leeve out in the cold yer Amerken Expressos and yer Mastychargers!)

But the reel pollyution in Vennis ain't the peeple, it's them factrys outside the place over in Mestry that keeps usin up this float-in sitty's undyground water fer to run all ther boilers and steem injins. Then ther's all the pollyution brung in by oiled tankers, pluss all that pidgin gwano that's deecomposing yer marbel statutes. Between sinkin and stinkin, this bewdyfull watertown is in trubble.

Mebby Canda's hedded fur the same kinda fix. We mite end up as a nashnul park fer the resta the wirld fer jist ten weaks of the yeer, then go on the pogey fer the uther forty-two, cuz not that menny tooryists likes to stay and play in the hale and sleet'n slush. It's awreddy happen in Vennis and Ire-land and yer hylands of Scotlan, not to mensun parts of our Martimes, wen mosta the yung peeple has to go away fer to find a job in greener feelds. Will that tern our country into a buncha retiredmint villedges fer seenery sittizens hoo cant afford to moove to Florider?

Visitin' a Venitian cat house

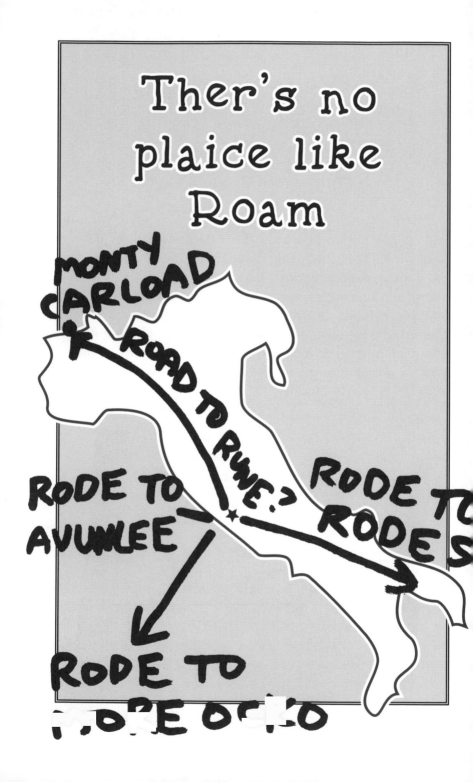

# The Interminal Sitty

Funny thing about Ittly, everybuddy goes by VIA, but VIA ain't yer rail like in Canda, it's yer rode. Eyetallyuns has bin callin' their rodes that sints the decline and fallout of yer Roaming Umpire. And that's well named, cuz them old-time Eyetalians roamed as fur as Ire-land. So if yiz want to take a bus yuh calls up yer VIA, not yer Voyeur peeple, like at home. And as the old sayin sez . . . all VIAS leeds to Roam. But we didden wanna be led to Roam. Even Valeda figgerd on brakin' our unbillical cord with our fella travlers. After chasin our bus allover Yerp and then chasin our gide allover Veenis, we deesided us Farquharsons peferred travlin solo ta bein in a convoy. We tole them we wuz off ta git lost agin (but this time we kep ahold of our luggridge) and we struck out fer Roam on our own. Valeeda wuz so parshill to that Orientail Expresso that she wanted to intrain herself all the way to yer Terminal Sitty. That's wat they calls Roam . . . sounded more like a busstop or a airport than a trane deepoe, but Valeda wuz bound and deetermine to git rode outa Watertown on a rale.

I think she's sorry now, cuz that train tern out to be more like a slubway ride. I'd herd quite a bit about yer Eyetalian undyground during World War Eleven, but I didden reelize they run the railroads so that travlers is kept mostly in the dark. Most of the jurny tord Roam is that way, even in daylite. Valeda thinks it wuz thunk up by sum showvizness mail prig so he could sectionally harse his fella femail passengers. She sez you take the time it takes fer to git thru one of then long tunnels, yiz cood have yer way with sumbuddy and nobuddy wood be much the wizer as to hoo it cooda bin. Valeda and I helled onto eech uther fer deerlife, and bein seezonal travlers by now, kep the uther hand on our wallits.

The tranes in Ittly runs on time like that Fashist dicky tater Musseleeny had sed they wood. Sumbuddy wanted to hall our luggridge fer us when we got off in Roam, but he wanted to charge us a thousand leerys per yer bag. We later found out that amount to about sexty-five cents so we shooda let him perseed with Operation Hernya.

Wun thing about Ittly, they may be short of sum things, but they'll never run outa paper. Wen I cash in wun of our Amer-ken Expresso travel checks, I shooda rent a weel-barrer fer to carry all them leerys I got back.

I wanted to git strait to our hotel witch wuz locate at the top of yer Spanish steppes. (Don't ask me wat Seniors and Senior Eaters wuz doin' in Ittly.) But insted of goin' strait to our lodge-ins, Valeda ast the tacksee fella to take us to yer Trivial Founting, cuz she had seen sum moovy yeers ago, and that wuz the furst thing to do. Tern yer back and throw sum munny over yer shoulder into the pool, and yer garnteed to git back to Roam sumday and spend a lot more munny. All this before we had maid up our minds if we liked the place in the first place! It wernt far to git there and we ended up in a square called a Pizza, witch is odd becuz Pizzas is genrully round.

Three cones at the founting

Wile Valeda threw her munny away I went and bot us sum jillatys, witch is Eyetalian fer icecreem, and the best thing about this hole country. I brung her one, along with the 2 fer me, and she took my pitcher . . . "Three Cones at the Founting." It wuz hard to git enuff elbow room fer her to flash on acconta all them dam tooryists. Wen we got back in the hack, squarshed in tween all our luggridge, the driver insest on showin' us the resta the blaim sitty, so ther we wuz peering at snatches of Roam between our snatchells.

Roam is bilt on 7 hills, and I think this driver wuz deetermin to take us on every one of them. He sure took us, all rite. We went to yer Roaming Form, but there wernt no hocky game on, so we druv past yer Baths of Cackacola ware I wuz temted to use yer Mensroom. Yer Colassalinoleum looked to be pritty rundown, even morn the one at yer Canadian Nashnul Exhibitionists in Trawnta ware the wife used to show her caffs in the big ring. This old Roamin roon got no roof and it look like it's never had one. Them sides is pritty bear too. Then we tackseed round yer Palenstine Hill ware the Umpeerial Impurers like Gustus Seizure used to live, and on to yer Sirkus Maxymouse, witch didn't seem to have any of its three rings goin'.

Wen Valeda sed she wuz anxious to go to the Vatica Can, I tole the driver to hed rite fer our hoetell cuz I needed to go too. He tuck us to yer Hotel dee Veal. Then the tacksyman ast us fer a hunderd thousand of leerer, and he wanted a good tip asswell. So I give him a good one: I tole him to take his cusstummers strait to their hoetel insted of a grantoor of all the Roamins-in-their-Gloamin sites.

The majer Doehoe at yer Hoetell de Veal, wen he wuz carrion our luggridge inside, tole us that wat we had cum in wuz not a regler cab, but a mavrick, and that we shoodna pade all that munny to sum Barbary Aryan hoo didden even have his cab licensed fer to cheet tooryists.

After we check in and compleated our toilets, we had our first Roaman meel. I noe now why they calls it yer Hotel de Veal. That's about all they have on their menyou. No spigetty and meetbawls or even a Pisa in site. So Valeda order up a Seezyer Sallid with a plait of Veal Scalpedpeenis.

I wuz gonna have sum Ozzy Bucko (Veelnuckles) but insted I went vedgy-aryan with sum kinda paster call Fetid-sheeny All-afraido. Valeda's sed her dredded veel cutlits wuz deelishus, and she warsh them down with sum Caffy Lada (witch sounded to me like a Roosiancar). My pastyer plate taist okay too, but it tern out to be nuthin' but Cheesy Marconi. I wuz gonna ast fer the bill but Valeda beet me to it, lookin up in her How-to-Speek-Lattin book, she sed "Eel Condo! Pray go!" Sounded pritty fishy to me and I wuz afraid we wuz gonna end up with a Roam townhouse on our hands.

And you mite a thunk that wuz the case wen the bill cum! Anuther hunnert thousand learys! Wurst of all, I found they had charge me 18,000 learys (eleven dollars sexty sents in reel munny) fer my meezly helpin' of Krapt Dinner!!

# Sites fer Soar Feet

Roam is pritty much an R.C. town, incloodin' yer Pope, and they got more churches even than Tronto. Fer a Yewnited Churcher, Valeda seemed to have a unholey intrust in yer Cathlick Church. If she wuz home in Parry Sound I dout she'd walk acrost the rode fer to see all them saints in ther nitches, even if ther wuz a Bingo throne in. But the first place my Proddistint wife wanted to git to nex mornin' wuz his Holeness's place of work, Sin Peeter's, witch is also Jonpall I Yi's lokel parrish. In fack, this Puntiff has got a regler sitty all to hisself rite inside yer Roaming Walls. Frum the outside, Sin Peeter's is a dedringer fer that Angle-can church over to London, Sin Palls. I figger the Roam one musta cum first tho. After Martin Loofa naled his feeses on the Widdemburgers' church door, he musta maid off with a lotta loot fer to git start up his own Baptist-Pressebyterian church. As the old sayin goes, he probly robbed Sin Peeter's to pay fer Sin Palls.

Us Prodderstants cooden have carted much away tho, cuz Sin Peat's is still pritty stuffed with statutes of plasterd saints way tallern basky ball players, about 18 foot. Also the biggest pullpit I ever seen, and abuv it the gold chare ware himself sits. Not too eezy to see yer way round in the corners cuz the place is lited oney by little candels, and it'll cost ya if yiz wants to git lit.

So the wife and former sweetart hedded fer yer Vaticacan Artsy Galley witch is called yer Sixteenth Chapple. This wuz chockablox to the dores, stand-in room only. I'm sure glad Valeda didn't wanna go thru the uther fifteen chapples. We stud behind a cuppla tooryists frum Taxes hoo musta bin in the middle of sum infeerior deckarating cuz they kept lookin' at all them big paint-ins on the walls, and wundrin' if summa them mite be too big fer their frunt rooms.

I never seen sitch big pitchers! And they cuvverd everything frum yer Cremation of the Universal to yer Lost Jedgement. The ladder wuz compleatly cuvverd over with a tar-palling. Valeda sed they wuz cleenin' up ther dirty pitchers, but I jist think them as is in charge of things don't want ya to see what's gonna happen to yiz at the Last Strumpet, cuz most peeple don't like sad end-ins.

Alla this paintin, every bored foot, wuz dun by one fella, Mike L. Anglo, hoo dun mosta the work lyin down on the job. He musta got a crick in his neck frum doin' it: I certny did tryna stare up at his stuff. My faverit of all them paintins wuz ware God gives Man the finger.

## Stoans of Roam

Today we deesided to void tacksy drivers and becum pederastrians on fut. It's a good thing we dun that, cuz ware we went the Vias wuz so narra that no veehicle cud git thru, eggsept mebby them Mope-Peds they call Vespers. Jist as well that all them Fee-ats and Masterottys and Alfalfa Romeos can't git everywares, cuz traffick in this sitty is more like that spring feeassco in Pamp-Loner Spane called "The Run-in With the Bulls." That's where they let them big horny aminals chase peeple up and down the streets, and that's morer less what the cars do here with ther horns.

Sum of them old streets like yer Via Happyer is the saim Roamin rodes that they used centurions ago fer ther old time taxis called litters. They had stricker traffical regglations in them days. Them sudan chairs was the only veehicles aloud in their daytime traffic jams. The carts and waggins fer the mark-its hadda cum in after sunset, wen Roam had no lites in them streets, eggsept yer own flair.

Valeda and I stuck to them liddle backstreets witch wuz overhung by bildins and seam as dark as yer pockit. I wooden call them streets as much as allies, the kind detached sitty peeple have between ther houses back home. And these slith-ery fut-paths ain't paved . . . they're cobbled with stoans. This musta bin wunna the oldist partsa town and I don't think them tennamints that loom over them had change much sints that book I red that wuz rit by a Gibbon, "Yer Deekline and Fallout of yer Roaming Umpire."

That wald-in feeling yuh gits in old Roam, it felt to me like I wuz back in yer B.C. instead of yer heer-and-now Anus Domineye. Accorn to that old Gibbon, Roam fell cuz all the hardup farmers wuz forced to moove inta town and git sum pogey and nobuddy wuz left to tend the craps. This cozzed yer problem of over-copulation, and them bildins jist kep gettin hire and hire on the same flimcy foundayshins. I'm not tockin wall-to-wall slums here, cuz rite nex door to a tennamint wood be a big mannerd-house with a courtyard inside and a fount-ing playing. No gettoes ware they packdige the poor. Yer rich patrishuns and yer poor plee-be-ins lived side by side, then as well as now. But Gibbon's sadistics sed that fer every big house there'd be twenny-six thousand apartments. It's still yer case in downtown Roam today, eggsept that the more ainshint bildins looks more modren than yer noo-fangel!

I wunderd wat them old Roam hi-rizes places wuz like inside, but Roamins spends mosta ther daytime lives outside ennyways. Seems to me frum wat I seen in these streets that these Medium-terranian peeples do the same things outdores that we do to home. To watch the locals washin', shavin', pluckin' chickins, feudin', fussin', and fightin' rite in fronta ya . . . it's sorta yer Grandole Roam Opry without the music. Sept the music is in their voices . . . ya'd sware they wuz all singing opry without instrymints, more like acupulco.

There's a reezin fer all them fountings in yer pizzazzas. Them old time Roamins had a sistern of akwee-ducks witch brung water frum miles away that wuz one of the seventeen wunders of the wirld. But it never got as far as them Roamins as lived on the secund floor and on up. The landlards lived on yer groundfloor and had run-in water and drainedge of ther soo-age, but

A breef rain in Roam

ther tennints abuv wuz jist S.O.L. (pardon my French). Them soors wuz so big yuh cood drive a hay-waggin thru em and not touch the sides, but it didden do much fer yer second story bunch. So they had a longer way to go to go, if yiz catch my meen-in. Mind yew ther wuz a lotta pubic latreens on the streets with marbel seets and marbel statures too, but it cost ya at leest a pritty penny. So most old-time Roamins bots a earthywair jar and tuck it downstairs every mornin to the sess-trench outside. The hire up yuh went the less you pade fer rent. Sum classless louts wood heeve-hoe ther jar's contense out the winder frum grate hites. I'll take life on the farm thank yew, ware the leevins stays at ground level and we spreds them around our land, not our dwellins.

No runnin water above yer groundfloor ment a lotta fires. It wuzn't that there wuz a lotta arson around, it's jist that wat kep them Roamins in heet wuz about as deefishunt as their waterworks. Ther wuz neether fireplaces ner fernisses so the only sentral heetin wuz a fire in the middel of the floor. That's why them slop jars cum in handy fer to put out. So much fer yer urbain hites of civilly-ization . . . no heet, no lite, no water and if yiz don't mind me tockin slop, cuvver yer hed wen yuh wock outside.

The wife's cussin Norman at werk in Room

We did git to see the inside of wun of them urbane palisses wen we found out the wife had relayshins in town. That Canajun moovie drector Normal Jewison is a Drain on his muther's side jist like Valeda is on her father's, and he wuz makin' moovys to send back to Hollowood ware all the lemmins cum frum. We seen the brite lites down by yer Tibber rivver, and folleyed ther glair till we got rite thair. Ther wuz Norm a-settin' rite on a dolly (not wat yiz think) and tellin' a buncha acters wat to do. He never seen us, but his wife Dicksee wuz thair and she invit Valeda and me to cum and watch and have supper with them afters in their rental plotzo not too fur away.

Fer a paliss it look pritty rundown on yer outsides, but pritty richy on yer insides. Valeda wanted to heer about all the peeples she reeds about in Peeples magzeen, but Norm he wanted to tock farmin cuz he has a two hundrd aker spred hard by Caledon and is prouder of his prize bulls and his mable seerop than his move-in pitchers. So we settle in fer a nice down-homey eevenin, ther in a paliss in Imperious Roam.

## Sardy Nite Live . . . Yer Baths

If yer avradge upperstory lowerd-class Roamin hardly had a pot to pee in, how in the sam hill wuz he gonna take keer of the resta his boddy wen it cums to yer hyjeens? Don't worry. All that import water in yer Akwee-ducks didden go to waist. The Roam idee of nashnul helth care wuz to take a bath. Not in the fountings, ware sum Roamins even today wash ther dogs, or even their cars, but in a grate big guvmint bildin cremated by the Sennit or the Impurer, jist fer the purpuss of rinzing yer private parts in public.

How much did it cost? A haff a cent! So even amung yer down and outers hoo had beggar-all ther wuz no sitch thing as yer Grate Unwashed. And like a Roamin Hollyday Inn, the kids got in fer free. This wuz deekreed by Seezer A-Gripper about 33 B.B.C. Yer men's parts and yer wimmen's wuz kep seprit until the Umpire went into its steep deekline under yer Impurer Neero. This wuz after the fire sail he held wen he maid an ash of downtown Roam. Valeda seen this in the moovy "Quo Vadis?" witch meens "Do I Noe Where I'm Going?" (After wondrin' around Roam the wife and meself kin sure git reelated to that!)

In the old time times, them baths wuz strickly fer peeple. They opend hard by noon and closed wen yer sun had set. I spose yuh cood make yer day in that place if yuh wuz unemploid. And hot and cole run-in water wuzn't all that wuz pervided to yer genial publick. They had Jims fer yer fizzicle jerks, massodge parlers fer to rub yiz the rite way, and even lieberries and mewseeyums, open to all John Q. Publicans in the most democrappic way. Even yer Emprer Hay-dree-un used to take time offa his throan fer to mingle with his subjecks in a sitzbath.

Havin' a Roamin bath

So them Roamins cood be fizzically culcherd and intelleckshully curious at the same time. And they plaid with therselfs in all kinds of games. Ther wuz tennis with the pam of yer hand (the rackets cum along a lot later, frum Sissly), or handbawl agin the wall, or role a hoop with a liddle hookstick, or even swingin both ways with the Dumbells. Restlers and restleresses got a grip on therselfs in the nood after smeering eech udder with oil and wacks to make ther skins more soople. This idee cum frum Grease witch had cremated yer Olimprick Games with, I gess, no corpulent sponsers perviding a budgit fer woredrobe. Yer Nikes, yer Reebucks and yer Deedass cum along a lot lader.

Mind you, ther wernt no mix rassling. Them saxes wuz sedge-gregated so ther wuz nun of yer sectional harsement. It wuz Hay-dree-un pulled yer sexes apart in the baths by puttin' up differnt times fer mennen wimmin. Wimmin cum erly, and the men staid lader.

Yer bath had fore parts to her. First yer dry Turky bath fer yer swetters, kinda like yer Finnisht Sonna, witch steem open yer pores. Then cum a second bath witch wuz almost as warm, but you sprinkled the water on and scrape them pores with a sumthing called a striggil (felt like a corncob maid of stoan). This wuz diffycult to do to yerself, so if yuh wuz stinkyritch ya brung along sum slave hoo wood git yiz abraysiv. Thurdly, yuh went into a Teppid-dairy'um witch wuz lukey-warm, and forthly and finely you took the plunj in a cold pool, yer Friggidairyum, so you went all the way frum bein in heet to froze in wun swell foop. Sum Roamins dun this morn wunce a day. Mebby that's why histerians say the reel reezin yer Roaming Umpire fell wuz frum its peeple takin' too many baths, witch maid them all go soft.

# Yer Roman Meel

Yer aftermath of yer afterbath wuz dinner. Mebby that's why yer ainshint Roamin wood always lie down fer his evenin meel, his mussles wuz too loose frum bathin' fer to sit up and take nurshmint. This wuz the only seeriuss meel of the day, even tho' yer avridge sittyzen had probly breefly entrenched hisself too or three times afore that. But they wuz liddle, cold stand-up, fast fud meels. Sum breckfusts wuz nuthin' morn a passing thing like glassa wotter. Lunch wuz mebby breddin cheez, warsh down with a liddle whine. This wuz offen taken on the huff, so most Roamins didden sit down . . . parn me . . . lie down . . . to table, till ther day wuz dun. To eet sittin up wuz felt as sumthin fit fer childern. To take it lyin down wuz consider more ellygunt and sofistificated. A lotta our peeple today git into a semi-reecumbrance posishun, but oney cuz they wanna watch with their TeeVee dinners.

Gests wuz pervided with die-vans on witch they laid themselfs crotchwise. Sum of them couches cood lay six or seven at a time, and mebby ate or nine with a pinch. They tuck off ther Roamin scandals and had ther feet warshed by a slave, even if them pedal parts wuz all-a-rinkle frum soakin in a bath haff the day. Nives, spoons and tuthpix wuz handed out, but notta fork in site! The only prongs were ther fingers, witch is why they hadda keep ther hand in ther fingerboles freekwent.

If yuh wuz smart yiz brung along yer own nappykin, so's you cood take away extry tit bits home in a dawgybag. The big-time Roamin lie-down orjy consist of sex or seven corses with mebby a intercorse in between fer to rest. That's wen the tables wuz turned and reeplace by uthers fer to git yer just desserts. Belching wuz considerd bein' plite to yer hostass, and braking wind wuz considerd takin' good care of yer helth. If yiz et too much, ther wuz always a liddle room nex door fer to releef yerself. I'm not talkin' about yer privvy, the Roamins oney had them in public. I'm tockin' about a speshul re-gurge place called yer Vomitory-um ware you went to give yerself the finger down the throte before yiz went back at it agin.

If yer wundrin why I noe so much about Roaman meels, it's cuz I had a seven corse dinner out to Tivvly, jist outsida Roam, ware the fountings play and a lotta modren Roamins still do too. The restrunt wuz called yer Sibble-uh . . . NOT naimed after them Servints that works fer the guvmint. I looked her up in yer Funken Waggonalls, and a Sibble is a ain-shint woeman hoo got inspired by sum lokel god to deliver proffit-seas out of the orafiss of an orkle.

Well sir, that'd be Valeda, fer she wuz sure inspired that nite wen she gimme a sprize party fer to celibate our farteeth analversary in Holy Acrimony. It wuz a wet nite so we cooden eet outside ware the fountings pass their water, but we had a toasty fire nex to our table fer to keep us in dry heet. Firstoff they serve us sumthing I had bin missin frum my spigetty ever sints I cum to Roam . . . liddle sweetish meety balls. Then cum fresh mushyrooms marionnated in Olive Oyl and dresst with sum kind of waterd crest. Nex cum liddle white cheezy balls that look like they cood be use fer ping pongs. They wuz called Rick Cotters and taist deelishus. Then hoemaid Slommy, so spicey it maid yuh spacey. I warsh this down with sum fizzy- less water wile Valeda fergot her W.C.T.U. pledge and had a dry wite whine.

On cum three kinds of pasters, and I tride them all: a fet- tid sheeny with fresh bazzle, then sum Ravvy Oley that taist like nuthin' I ever had outa yer Sheff Boy Hardy, and finely sum paster that looked like liddle eers dropt into spinitch. Then afore yer mane corse cum yer intercorse . . . toast with a hole garlick on a stick fer to rub it in. Folleyed by roast lam with fresh geenbeens and uvvin-roast taters with Rose Murry. And wat did we warsh all that down with? SHAM PAIN!

After that cum yer peesa resistunts. I never thot Eyetalians wuz big on desserts, sept fer ther iced creem. Ther best noan contempuary deesert is called Anglish soop. Yuck! Even them old-time Roamins tuck it eezy on therselfs by dessert time . . . they settle fer a peesa froot, like apples'n pairs, or graips. But not Valeda Drain Farquharson . . . no siree, sirrah . . . not fer bobsnuts. She musta confurd with the Sibble-a kitchin cuz they womp up the best finisher I ever taisted . . . it's called Buckoney Dollcheese . . . and it's lite as yer perversial fether bein' mostly wip creem and ma-rang with fresh razz and blew burys. As them Roamins likes to say, it were Ammonia fer the Gawds.

To have hot chess nuts and a lickyer called Amretto wuz kinda yer Aunty's climax, becuz by that time I wuz stufft enuff to be mounted by a taxi-dermis.

# Playin Games:
# The Gory That wuz Roam

Seams that Roamins of old wuz oney intrusted in two things . . . bred and sircusses. So hoo ever wuz in charge of them maid sure that ther subjecks wuz fed and amewsd. It kep ther minds offa pollyticks.

Nowadaze our contempuary Common Housers gives us pollyticks instedda bred but ther perseedins still looks like yer averidge sirkus. They give us soors and new prisms fer ther big sociable projecks. But them Roamins wuz even more sociabull. They worked less and had more Festerals than any uther bunch in histry.

Wen the Romans wuz all Republicans the candiedates fer yer Sennit wood put on games fer to win votes. And wen Roam becum Imperiuss, them Emprers wood give everybuddy holly-days jist to keep up ther aleegions to Roam.

I dunno how enybuddy cood ern much bred cuz they wuz all on hollydays 159 times per anus, witch is mosta the yeer! A lotta workers nocked off every day at noon, and ther wuz anuther hunnert thousand got nocked off all the time cuz they wuz sudsidized by pogey. So peert neer everybuddy deepended on the Emprer's large-ass.

These heer Festerals wuz sposed to be deevine in orejin, but the messes of peeples oney caird about havin' a gud time. Them in charge peefurred that to havin them yawn thru ther lives. Peeples hoo start yawnin' start thinking about revlution, and you-noe-hoo finds things fer idol hands to do it to. Roam cooden keep 'em down on the farm, so they kep 'em outa the Roamin Form and give 'em every uther day outside a sircus like we duz nowadaze with sports on tellyvision.

At first them games wuz pritty strait forerd, copeed frum yer Geek Olimpricks. Boxing and fut races, jabbelin and discuss throwing, and even spouting pomes, but it never got poplar cuz yer avridge Joe don't roar and do the waves after jist heering a buncha verse. So the Sennit tuck a gambol and give them horse races, and they cot on fast, speshully in them big sulkys called charry-its. I seen them harness racists in that moovy "Ben Her," and it sure wuz eggsitement enuff fer me. But sitty peeple git jade pritty fast, and they need biggern bigger jolts fer to stirrup ther blud. So wen they went to the theeyater fer to see a stragedy (witch is a murder play) they started yellin' fer reel blud. And the mangement give it to them . . . in buckits. They got sum poor slave fer to take the actor fella's place in the last axe, and he REELY got the chop with no chants of comin' out fer to take his bow. This wuz the start of yer deekline and fallout.

But yer decadunces of the public got board with that too. So they put two of their amper-theeyaters together and desine a bildin strickly fer mass slotter . . . yer Roaming Colossalseamen. It cood seet 45,000 bludthirsty fans on all sides and anuther 5,000 hoo cood stand fer the hole thing.

The show wuz in the bole in the middel, jist like yer Make Beleeve Gardings. It wuz a big hit rite frum the start, cuz it give peeple wat they reely wanted to see . . . the deth of sumbuddy elts. The fiters wuz called Gladdy-aters and wuz recroot frum convicks, slaves, prizners of wore and most poplar of all, Christyuns. Sum of them glads wuz the rooned suns of grate famlys, and they even had their own agents, middlemen fer deth, to fix up fites fer them. They all becum Stars fer a Day.

The fore play was kinda like yer Gay Cups . . . there was a big bankit the nite before with haff of them fiters havin ther last meel. The Christyuns wernt invite to that—they staid in their cages with prairs and breddinwater. Then nex day ther wuz a Big Prade, with the gladdy-aters drest in purple and gold,

and they wuz druv round town in car-
rages with ther valleys (buttlers) runnin'
behind them on fut carryin' their weppins. Convicks with BUTTLERS! (These
fiters wuz mostly murderers, but once inside yer urena they
wuz popstars till deth. Put yiz in mind of today?)

The world premeer of this amewsmint senter wuz open by
Emprer Tite-ass. In his honner—and you'd wunder wat yer
Environly Mentalists nowadaze wood say to this—5 thousand
wile beests wuz destroid in one day: lines and tygers, bares and
elfunts, buffloes and rinosassserasses. Not to menshun peeple.
The Christyuns lost to yer Lion's Cubs 56-0.

The Emprer or his Emprass got to deesidde wether yer
loosers went on to the semmy finals or jist bot it rite then and
ther. Everything hung on ther Impeeriuss thums. Up . . . yer
spaired. Down . . . yer spair ribs.

The crowd luvved it wen Tite-ass put his thum down. And
this wuz how the morals of yer Roaming Umpire wuz con-
trolled fer morn two centurion by bein kept under one man's
thum. And them Christyun marters kept cumming (and going!)
till alluva suddint a mirrorkill happen. They convert a Emprer
to their side . . . Constant Teen. And he stopt them bloody
games all cold. The biggest thing left in that old roon of a bildin
today is a Cross.

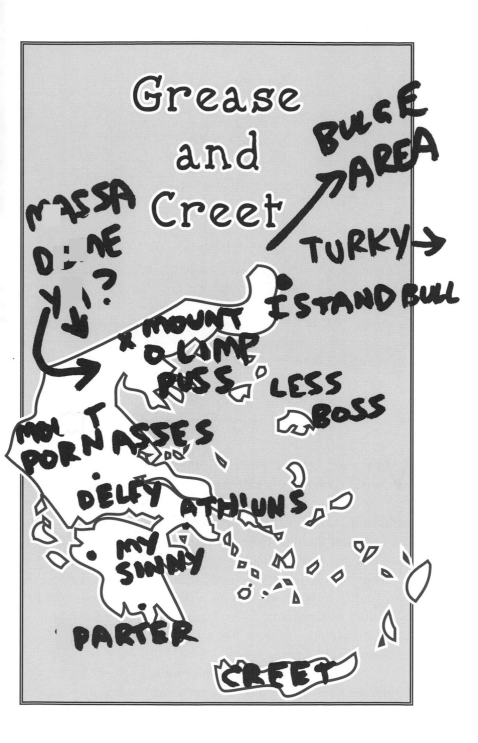

Deer Froot of our loins: Heer we are in Grease—witch remines me—don't fergit to ile the hay-bailer before ya starts cuttin' yer swath. This X marks our hoetell winder egpept that this card is the frunt and we are round the back. Are yiz gittin in the hay? Purrhaps yer gurlfrend cud helP ya. Luv Mummindad

# On to Grease

Valeda sez Athins wuz the littery capitol of yer old-time wirld. I bleeve it's still yer case, cuz I seen more litter in that town than anywares elts. Noizy too, with all them carhorns blairing. Mebby it wuzn't trafficking frusteration but the fack that them Geeks wuz about to axersize their french-frize in a federast election.

These're the fellas who started the hole ideer of demockercy, and frum wat I seen on the streets they seamed more het on it than us Canajuns. Every squaired incha space had bloo and wite banners flutterin like a Use Car markit on yer Dam Forth in Trauma, Ontaryo.

Our hoetell, yer Gram Bertannyuh wuz pure Grease, not Englitch like it sounded, but everybuddy seam to speek our langridge. It were rite acrost the rode frum ther Parlmint bildins, on wat they call Sin-Tag Muh Squair. If yuh craned yer neck a bit frum our sexth-flore winder, yuh got a glimps of yer Crappolis, a pritty rundown lookin naberhood rite up on toppa the town. On top of that bit a rubbel wuz a erly hy-rize called yer Parthy-nun witch looked like a rooned bank that had bin outa bizness fer sum time.

Ther wuz a wotter shortedge on in town at the time we wuz thair, and ther wuz a sine in our room with the suggestiv that we shooden shower aloan. Valeda snift and sed she'd take a bath insted. (I gess she figgers after farty years of holy acrimony we don't noe eech uther all THAT well.)

That nite we went to a restrunt reck-amend by the conchyurge of our hoetell. It wuz in a parta town called yer Placker, witch wuz fulla mostly sue-veneer shops. The restrunt had a big pitchcr of the cook over the frunt doore, and wuz called yer Taverner. Inside wuz fulla tooryists and almost as many waders. Valeda worn me not to drink the wotter, with or without Gaz, unlesson it caim in a boddle, so we order up a big flaggin of aitch-too-oh. It cum with the top alreddy off. Valeda tuck one sip and maida face. "It's nuthin' but tap wotter." Insted of wining to the mangement we orderd sum with a cap on it.

Ther's 2 kinda whines in yer Grease . . . Oozy-o and Recked-seena. The furst taist like lickerass, and the tuther taists like terpintime lace with Pine Sol. I settle on yer lickerass, cuz Valeda felt she wuz jist drinkin candy. Fer fud we start off with a Terror-me-salada, witch is fish paist loded with garlick. We had, I repeet, we had mammarys of it fer the nex weak.

Then we tride the lokel speshultys, cuz I figger if you wants things to be jist like home wen yer a brod, jist stay there. Valeda had Shiskey-bobs and I had Moose-a-ka-ka. Wun is meet on a stick and the tuther is mints stake with custerd. We finnish off with sum cheese that cum frum a gote. The menyou sed it wuz Fettid and I agree.

Rallyin'
round
ther flag

That dun it fer me, and the tapwater dun it fer Valeda so we hed back to the hoetell, but it tuck us a long time to git thair, fer yer Sintagme Squair wuz all got up like Nooyeer Seeve. It wuz a big plitickle rally fer yer Socialites under ther leeder Pappy Ann Drayo. He wuz the leeder of yer Oppsit Posishun tryna unseet yer Retrogressiv Conservativs hoose leeder wuz the present incumbrance.

I sware to yiz ther wer a millyun Geeks outside our hoetell marchin about and shoutin and wavin' their bammers, and car horns nunstop till three in the mornin. Makes our Canajun leedership prevenshuns look pritty taim. Nex day ther wuz litter on toppa the litter. And morn a bit a polly-ution too . . . wat they calls smug. Valeda and me wocked over to them old bildins on yer Crappolis needeep in bloon wite ribbings and plackerds.

She's a offal clime up to yer Partin'on, and it's even more rundown-lookin close up. Ther's no ruff overhed on this bildin, and everythin' on this roon looks bair as a bored. They use to have freezes and statchutes holdin up the ruff called katydids, but them Geeks lost all ther marbels to the Briddish over a centurion ago.

But the clime up she's wirth it if yer a demmycrat. Fer them Athins sittyzens wuz the first to bring up yer yooman rites of indyviddles, at a time wen everbuddy elts wuz eether a vassle or a ty-rant.

Valeda wuz nun too impress by them first demmycrats sints their wimmen was deafnitly secund class sittyzens. Feemails wuz clast with forners and uther aileens, and were a kind of slave in ther own rite, told by law to keep to home, barefut and preggerunt. And ware wuz the huzbins wen ther wimmen wuz doin the chores? Hangin' around yer pubic squairs tockin' fillosofees, or croozing down to the jim stairing at teenyage boys workin' out. Not jist stairin, but with a vue to gittin involv fizkly, so that a lotta these married men cood qualifry as batchlers of pederasty. They thot a boy's swett wuz sexier'n a girl's poorfume. Them old-time Geeks wuz nuthin' but by-sectional showviznist mail prigs.

After clime-in down frum yer Crappolis we went over to yer atey thousin seet Olimprick Stayjim, and it look bran new to me. Terns out it wuz oney ten yeer old. Yer orignal rig wuz up in a place called Olimpyuh witch is locate summers out in the Grease boondox. And so is most of what they call yer classy-ick tempels and statchels. So before we cum back to our hoe-tell we sined up at yer Geeker Torst Bored fer a bustoor of all them old places, startin the nex mornin.

Carryin a torch fer the next Olympics

That nite we didden sleep too good, cuz ther wuz anuther rally round yer flags, boys, this time put on by the guvmint farces hoo wuz Possessive Conservative. Ther wuz a thurd party splinter off frum yer Bloo Torys, but they never showed as fur as we cood see. This ring-dang-doo wuz even bigger and noiziern the wun the nite before. And honky!! Them cars never give up till three o'clock in the mornin with ther horny goins on.

Valeda and I stud on our balkany and watch it all. They had red flairs and fireworks witch sounded like a canon goin off. Valeda got a bit antsy in her pantsys cuz it seem less like a eleckshun than it did a Resolution! Meself I thot it wuz less like a hocky riot in Muntryall, and more like a Gay Cups futball rally, or Trawna celibating anuther Wirld's Serious.

# Yer Classy-Kill Toor

Nex mornin we wuz off to see old run-down naberhoods all over yer Grease. I look around me on the buss. Lotsa witeheds jist like Valeda and me. Beesides us seenery sittizens ther wuz a cuppla yung smoochy noolyweds, two married Maxycans floont in our langridge, and fore Japaknees spoke Anglish bettern yoon me (terns out they lived in Sam Fran Crisco). Valeda and me sat beeside a cuppla West keesters frum Vancoover, and we becum innimit fiends. They wuz hazbin and wife, and I sat with him. He musta bin a sockbroker or chartable accountant cuz all he tocked about wuz yer exchange rapes on our munny. I think he spent more time tryna git a quarter of a sent up on these furn bankers than he dun watching the sites go by.

Our toor gide wuz naim Kris Teen, and she innerduce us to our bustdriver, naim of Costus. (He never live up to his naim, tho', cuz he dun all our luggridge-liftin fer free.) Kris Teeny giv us all this histerical inflammation. Without her I wood never have seen nuthin' along the way eggsept vegetatin'.

We past a semitairy and it had yer odd sidepress, witch look like Chrissmuss trees all trussed up fer sail. Them partickler treeze is poplar in gravedyards cuzz the ruts don't disturb yer corpsus.

Wun of the hazzerds of livin' round here is not oney the shakey econmy, but yuh has to watch yer step fer all the erthquakes they has underfoot. They must have more falts in these parts than the wife thinks I has. The hole town of Cornth wuz rooned by wun of them big moovemints lesson a hunderd yeer ago. And the oney thing left standin in most of them old time classy-kill sites is colyums, witch tern out to be of three kinds . . . 1) yer Crinthian, witch is all leafy up top like a artsy choke; 2) yer Ironick, witch is curl up at the top like the ramshorn on a mounting gote; and 3) last but leest, yer Dorks, witch are jist as plane as the noze on my face.

We wuz heddin fer a penisinsular called yer Pulpyneezes, a lot more furtle than yer maneland. This is ware the old time Grease reely got started, naimly in a place called My Sinny. (I bleeve our boy Orville's gurlfrend has a poorfume called that.)

Back in yer classy-kill daze, the town of Corinth wuz ware it's at, the crotchroads of all Grease. Corinth deekline wen Athins cum up, but in its hay-days it wuz yer big Sin Sitty. But not like yer Hamsters Dam. This Corinth durty bizness wuz not oney offishully condoan sluttyness, but downrite reelijuss as well!!!

Valeda still don't bleeve it, but it's all troo. Yer lokel cherch wuz yer tempel of Afferdighty, yer godass of luv'n bewdy, and this so-call holey place wuz servissed by 1,000 preestasses, all of hoom wuz prosty-toots. These lokel gurls, no bettern they shood be, give the munny they got in trade back to the cheef preest of ther tempel, and fer that reezin they wuz all pureyfride and reddy to start up agin in the bizzyboddy bizness. That preest today weeda call nuthin' butta pimp.

No wunder Sin Pall sent a cuppla strong letters to them Crinthee'uns after his visit there. Ther's no trace of that big brothill of a tempel with a statchure of Afferdighty-without-no-nighty. But the gide showed us the stoned stump ware Sin Pall preeched agin all this as he wuz tryna git the lokel girls over the hump and into the troo fathe. Wile Pol (reel name Sol) wuz in town he got put in the lokel hoosedgow fer his Christyun thots. But this wuz duran yer Roaming Occipation, and Pall wuz let go cuz he wuz a Roaming sittyzen. He staid 18 munths and maid a bair livin' in the tents bizness, but went on to Fillups-pie to convert uther preeverts. Lookin at all them Orfadocks Bizzyteen churches roundybouts I'd say Sin Pall cum out on top.

Lemme tell yiz one thing. Nun of yer contempuary Grease peeple bleeves in enny of them old-time gods. This land is compleatly cuvvered with liddle Orfadocks churches with red tile roofs, all of them crossed on top. They is hunnert preesent Christyuns and they think us tooryists is crazy to go bussing all over lookin at a buncha paygun tempels that ain't even hardly thair ennymore.

And no wunder. Them ainshint gods wuz a absoloot dissgrace, and not werth warshippin in the furst plaice. They wuz no bettern yoon me, and I don't noe about yoo, but I'll betcha them dee-uh-titties wuz probly a hole lot wurse. You take that hed god of thers, yer Zoose, you'd expeck him mebby to make a eggsample of hisself. Nosirree Bob. He wuz a regler caution. Furstoff, he insested on marrying up with his own sister,

Startin' the Odd-sissy in Grease

Heera, and ever after cheeted on her with both sexies to a farthy well. Hera sed her hazbin tern out to be a immoral nimf, but she wuz no angle herself, she got into her adultryhood pritty fast. No wunder them Geeks never had no ten commandmints, cuz their gods never forbad nobuddy nuthin', speshully therselfs.

You'd wunder wat Zoose and Hera's pairents wooda thunk about these derangemints. Mummindad wuz called yer Tite'uns, probly cuz they had a drinkin problem. Zoose's Dad wuz old Crownose, and his Muther was jist noan as Oops. (Mebby she spilt a lot.) These two old soakers didden have no pairints to speek of; they jist seem to cum outa Kayoss wun nite.

The scandles bout this hevvenly gang outdoos yer Gnashnul Sink-quirer. Zoose had oney a cuppla childern to speek of, the resta them wuz a buncha little basterds. Oney childern he ever had by Heera wuz Marse, yer God of bluddy Wore, and Vulkin, god of fire and hevvy mettle (he tern out to be a topnots blacksmitt). Heera clame she had him all by herself (if yiz kin conseeve of sitch a thing)—nuthin to do with Zoose, witch is mebby why the boy wuz allways in the doghouse with Zoose, and that's why they nickednaim him Plutoe.

Zoose's faverit oftspring wuz Atheeny, hoo he clame wuz borne of no muther, but sprung frum her Dad's fourhed waring full armer. Zoose had anuther dodder called Afferdighty, yer blond Veenis and sex goddass of luvvin' bewdy. She wuz sposed to hav bin conseeve outa the fome of yer see. I'm sure this never fool Zoose's wife enny more than it duz you or me. Then ther wuz Artymiss, the reesult of anuther of Zoose's bits on the side, hoo becum a mitey hunter with boas and arras and wuz sumtimes noan as Dye-anna, Gert with a Quiver. Sounds to me like a drink problem.

Her twin bruther wuz A-polo, also big on archyree, as well as playing with his lyers, so he wuz in charge of fizzical and uther culcher. Uther suns wuz Hermys (his Romain name wuz

Murky) god of currier survisses, flour deliverer, and partime theef on the side. But last at leest, the chip offa the hole block and Zoose's particler mail pick a the litter, wuz Dye-a-nice-ass. This wuz his sun outa sum Theebs prinsass, Semelly. He wuz a ring tail snorter of a drinkin devvil if ever ther wuz one, and he becum god of Boos.

Wen I tole our busstoor Girl Gide I didden bleeve all that bull about Zoose (esspeshly the story bout him ternin into a aminal), she sed it wuz a mith, but a mith wuz as good as a mile wen it cum to goin' the distants in peeples minds. She sez it's kinda like Sandy Claws, and our mith about him goin round the wirld in one nite bringin everybuddy sumthin. I tole her that a lotta kids loose intrust in Chrissmuss wen they lern Sandy Claws is a mith, and tramsfer their a-legions to Bocksing Day. She sed her peeple feels the same about classic-kill Grease and the oney paygun god gits much warship nowadaze is that wino, Dyin Ices. His survices is helled mostly on weak ends.

# Yer House of Hate-Wee-Us

Tock about a dis-funky famly, them old time Gawds had it all over our own House of Wincer's "Chuck and Die" brigaid. And that goes dubble fer the Roiled famly of yer House of Hate-we-us that wuz our next stop on yer Pullapeneezers. Them Roils wuz a downrite pubic mennis. The flounder of the famly, Hay-tree-us, give the chop to his neffuse and neezes, then fed them to ther dad (his own bruther) in a stoo on account of that saim bruther had sedooce Hay-tree-us's wife. So the bruther stop fooling around with his sistern-law and had a sun by his own dotter, the oney wun that didden end up in the stoo.

The sun grew up to chop his Unkel Hate-ree-us up, and put his ole man on his throan insted. That neff-you coodna last long cuz Haitreeus sun, Aggie Memnon tuck back the throan. Aggie wuz alreddy infamuss wen he sackerficed his own dotter, Iffy-Deny-yuh, before he went off fer ten yeers wirth of baddles in Troyland. Ya kin reed all about this in a book called yer Ill-eeyad (sounds kinda sick ta me).

Wen Aggie Memnon cum back demobbed, he got merder his first nite hoam by his own wife Clitternester and her wore-time luvver, the saim fella had nocked off Aggie's pop. I ast Valeda if she'd ever herd the like of that in them Tabbyloids she reeds wile waitin in line at the Soupymarkit. Valeda sez she never herd of sich goins on eggsept in them soapy oprys on the TV. This hole House of Hate jist seem like Another Wirld to her.

Ware all them bluddy things happen wuz rite in frunt of us, in a paliss on the tuther side of yer Lyin Gate. Mind, the Roiled Paliss now looks more like a rut seller, but Aggie Memnon's toom is all there, thirty foot hy in consenting sirkles like a big beehive. It's yer CNN tower of Mysinny. But ther wernt nobuddy ded put up in it. Our gide figgerd that Aggie's wife probly fed her old man's boddy insted to the dogs. It gimme the creeps to be hangin round

At yer
(non-
Vancoover)
Lyin Gate

Valeda plays a matnay in Eppy Doorus

this house of creeps, so I wuz kinda releeve wen we got back in the bus with sum live ones.

Our buss-gide cheer us all up by tellin us she wuz takin us to the theeyater. She dun it too, but ther wernt no show on. Valeda thot ther hadden bin enny sints mebby three thou yeers but that's not troo. They still have summer Festerals (Fryday and Sardy nite live), jist like we duz with Stratferd-on-Tario and yer Pshaw. But this theeter at Eppy Doorus wuz forteen thou seets all open to yer airs, more like a haffa-Skydoom without the distractable roof.

Eech summer heer they puts on the same old Geek shows they used to millenemas ago: stragedys, witch is sad plays by Easekillus, Soppy-klees and Youripadees, along with the odd fartsical comdee by a funny fella with a even funnier naim, Hairystuffyknees. And I'll betcha yuh kin heer every word in the back rose, cuz we tride it with me 200 foot away up in the cheepist seet and Valeda down frunt singin "I've No Bizness in Show Bizness." Our gide sez the old place has purrfick acoostinks, witch is wat I sweep out of our barn twice a day.

After Valeda sung, we all went to the hospiddle. It's the oldest in the hole of yer wirld so nacherly it's in roons, but that's wat the pessaryists say about our own sociabilized helth skeem. This old rotted hospiddle is now a sankchewairy dessicated to the God of Heeling, Eezyclappyus. It still smells jist like a hospitable, mostly on accounta all them fur trees givin off their Pine-sol musk. I dunno if I'd ever have want to be treet there, cuz wile yuh wuz asleep they used to use snakes fer to lick yer woons. Mebby that's why doctors lowgoes always got serpints crawlin up their pole. If Valeda had seena reel snake, she wooda bin the one crawlin' up the pole.

# Fuss-In, Fude-In and Fight-In

We wuz back on the buss without too much fuss and we wuz drivven thru Arkadia, witch naim sound to me like parts of Noo Brunsick and Novy Kosher, but Valeda sed it's the part of the wirld that priddy pomes is most writ about, with nimfos and sheepherds dancin' on a lawn that looks like a billyards tabel.

Well, them potes has not kep up with modrin devellupmints cuz yer Arkaid is now wun of the poorst parts a Grease, and emty too, havin bin mostly abandon by mosta their inhibitants rite after World War Eleven. (Them as wuzn't nocked off in sibble wores or fudes.) Oh them Arkadians wuz regler hillbillies gunnin fer eech uther jist like yer reel Mickoy and yer Hatfield. Every nooborn kid wuz consider as a extry gun in the family. They wooda fit rite in round our parts today.

We drove thru a cuppla goastowns that look desserted. Before we noo it, we wuz out of Arkadia, and goin thru Sparter, and didden the gide give us a eerfull about that bunch! They wuz top dogs in Grease fer bout five hundert yeers mostly by bein the lokel bullys. They had no use fer book lernin, and even ther laws wuz never writ down . . . words wuz ennemies to them.

They wuz strickly dung-ho fer unyversal millinery serfice. Ther wernt no other jobs aloud fer the yung but gittin in unyform and follying orders of yer speerier offiser. The Spartin kids wuz took frum ther muthers frum the age of seven and lived in a army barks, but spent most of ther time bivvywhacked outside on yer cole cole ground! If a baby looked like he or she wernt too helthy it wuz left outside to exposure therselfs.

Them Sparters had no truck with forners, and never let ther yuths travel anywares elts. Funny thing wuz that wen Spartuns finely broke outa home and harth, and got a umpire overseized, bang went all ther dissiplin. They went to pot and tuck the first bribe that cum along, and evechly they deeklined and fell out jist like them Roaming Umpires.

Wat Sparter is best reememberd fur is leevin' nuthin' beehind. Not even roons. Nuthin' werth lookin' at, our gide tole us so we never stopt. Them Sparters never cared a stinker's dam fer mewsick or statchyews or pomes, oney fightin' and eetin three squairs a day, and that don't add up to a civilly-ization. Jist bair slubsisterns. That's why today ther ruts is no wares to be seen, and ther's no post cards fur sail. So ther hertage is nothin to rite home about.

But let's give 'em ther dooze. They dun a bang up job of keepin off them Purrzian hords at Thermonopoly, wen every blaim one of them dide eggsept the fella excaped to carry the noose back home. And they did stop ther 27 yeer war with the Athens bunch fer five daze every fore yeers fer to take part in yer Olymphical Games. This wuz wair we wuz on our way to next.

Them first-time Games wuzn't held over to O-Limp-Yuh atall, but hard by Turky at yer Troy. Accorn to Hoamer, the old blind sneer as rit yer Illy-Ad and yer Oddsissy, them games wuz downrite fewneeryill at first. They start up as a kind of "wake yer ded" celibation. Seems that the hevvywate champeen of yer Geeks, A-killus, lost his boyfriend Pet Rockless wen he wuz Hectord in a ambush by a packidge of Trojans.

Insted of cryin in his bier, A-killus set up a wake-up party insted. Sounds kinda Ire-ish, don't it? Ther wuz prizes fer the winers in boxin, rasslin, discos, charryit racists, upchucking yer speer, throwing the java and herling yer biscits. It give them unyform boys sumthin to do wen they wasn't sackin, pillow-gin' and lain waist.

# O-Limpyuh

O-limpyuh is lushus compair with the resta yer Pulpypeenises. They even got wotty mellins, shugger cains and bambooze. O-limpyuh's vally is a bewdyfull site, and wen yuh git off yer buss, all that green around yuh makes yuh feel at peeces with yerself. But this site wuz morn jist fer yer athaletic supporter. It wuz a reelijuss sankchewairy ded-dickate to Zoose, yer god of piece. (Deepends how ya spells it.) It tuck fifty yeer to bild Zoose's tempel, and ten yeer fer that sculper Fideous

Let the games begin!

to git off a statchyou to him thurty foot high with a ivery boddy and a gold dress, and a silver reeth on toppa his hed. The hole thing sounds like a lamp the wife wood buy at a Wite Ellafint sail.

Most of Olimpyuh ain't here enny more. Sum of it's in Parse, Frans, and them Briddish had bin at it agin and took a shiplode of sooveneers. Thair's nuthin much to see on yer ackshell plain feelds. The stayjim ware all the games wuz helled jist looks like wun of my feelds that's lyin falla. Ide say it wuz about ten aker in aria, but wen it cum to goin the distants, the Geeks maid wun Olimpick stayjim a eunuch of mezzuremint like . . . "We better ask Dad fer the charryit tonite, cuz this dants weer goin to is 300 stayjims away."

Mind, ther never wuz no seets round it. Forty thou peeple jist sat on ther arse on the ground. And no overnite plaices fer visiters to stay back then neether. Them athaletes wuz under cuvver in a Olimprick villedge cuz they cum a munth erly fer to trane. But the gaims therselves wuz oney five days, so all the expeckteraters jist sacked out fer the nite on Tairy Firmer. No problim. When we wuz here the ground wuz still as dry as a burd's A-hole in Awgist. But them La Goons wuz fulla muskitters, jist like back then, wen everybuddy kep prayin to the gods fer to git rid of the pesky things. So did we.

Valeda cooden bleeve her eers wen the gide tole us all them Olimprickers cum on fer their races undressed bair as a burd. Not oney them but ther trainers wuz in yer buffed asswell. No wimmen wuz allowed in eggsept the Hy Preestass of Dim Mutter, the Goddass of Furtilities. The nood rool wuz put in after sumbuddy's muther wanted to see her boy compeat in the gaims, and she cross-dresst. Wen the wind bloo up her roabs and showed she wuzn't a man of parts she wuz throwed out on her rear.

Ther wernt no bigger honner than cummin in first at yer Gaims. The hometown bunch use to tare down the walls fer to welcum ther heero, shoutin "Who needs de fence, we got us a

Olimfick meddler!" Sum of them kids with the reeths got pritty fulla therselfs, and evenchly . . . oh, oh! . . . heer cums the bribe! . . . soon they got munny fer winnin sted of a fissfull of oliv branch.

It didden take long until them winners wuz gittin' hiley pade like our base ballers today. After sponsers cum age-ints and pubic relayshins peeple. If yiz won at Olimpyuh then yuh went on toor and franchised yerself at uther games. Wen them Roamins got involv, the rot got rottner. Old time Geeks bleeved in play fer fun, but them Imperious Roamins wanted pay fer play.

Impurer Neero tride to git into the act, and fix the charryit race so's he cood win. He did too, even tho' he fell off twice and never even finnish! He got goaled meddled, but every-buddy that wuz on the spot noo it had bin Zeero fer Neero.

But uther cheeters never prosperd. Ther wuzn't any of them steereoids like in Souse Kareer ware a runner cood piss away a gold meddle, but it's on reck-urd that ther wuz 17 tramsgressers wun yeer and they all hadda offer up a statyou of Zoose and put on the boddem ther famly name to cumpound ther shame. And these cheeter statchutes wuz put

Enterin' the Olympic Hall of Shaim

up in frunt of yer entrants to the Olimprick Stayjim fer all passers-buy to give three jeers.

In reckrowspeck, wat gud wuz alla them gaims that went on fer hunnerts of yeers? Mostly plitickle. It nashnulized all them differnt sitty-staters so that they reelize that watever place they cum frum, they wuz all in yer Grease together. After beetin the craps outa eech other in baddle fer hunnerds of yeers, it wuz the five daze of peece of them gaims every fore yeers that evenchly got them sitty-state Greasers all together into wun nayshin.

# Gettin Our Filla Delfy

I ast our toorgide if she ever got sick of all this ainshint histry. She tole me no, it's her life werk, but she also tole me that the only histry that enny of her fella countrymen gives a dang about wuz wat happin in the last hunnert and sexty yeers. That's wen patter-erotick Geek party-zans started up yer wores of libberations agin their Turk overlards. She tole me all this on a fifteen minit fairy ride acrost yer Golfa Corinth at yer thurd biggest sitty in Grease, Patterass.

Our buss wuz hedded up to the most relijuss place in all old-time Grease, Delfy, on the sloaps of Mount Pornasses. The seenery round these parts is the most gorge-uss we seen so far.

Delfy is a yeer round torst attrackshun cuz they gits lotsa snow up yer Pornasses in winter. Jist as menny visiters are here then, but a lot yungern our bunch, cuz they're skeers, so ther hoetells is full all yeer. But this place has bin a big commershul venture sints time in memoriam.

It seams yer old time heethin thot of Delfy as the senter of the erth, the wirld's naval. They first new it frum a hole in the ground that give off a lotta gass. Then sumbuddy got smart and tern this gassy hole into a big commershul shrine. Got a neerby vergin hoo cood handel her gass to be preestass. She wuz all-ways called Sibble, no matter wat her naim wuz. She sat on a rock over this orfiss, inhail the stuff cummin up, and then babbeld away in a way that everybuddy thot she had all the ansers. And them visiters shure pade hevvy dews to heer wat she hadda say.

The thing wuz . . . ya never got a yessir-no anser frum them fewms . . . it wuz allways a kind of riddel rap up in a ennema. Fr'instants . . . wen yer Athins bunch ast wat wood help them beet off the evaders of yer Purzian Umpire, the anser wuz "woodin walls." So the sitty of Athins started puttin' up duh-fences round ther town. But it wuz ther navel fleat wat beat all them Purzian cats. So mebby wooden walls ment that if them Asstheenians deepend on ther fleat, them forn potent taits wood git the ships beeten outa them.

# Yer Creetins

Wen we got back to Athins today we sed goodbuy to all our fella bussers. Mosta them wuz off the nex day to see the eyelands of Grease, like Mickeynose, Deeloss, Nacksoss, Roads, Santa Reemy, Sidepress, Lessboss, and Patmass.

Valeda and me wuz hedded fer Eejippt and our girl gide tole us we shood take a one day sidestrip to Creet witch wuz dreckly in our way. Creet had bin a civillyization even before yer Grease, went back five thou yeers, and had a hunderd sit-tys with ladies drest in hy fashyun (bare teated with WASP wastes!) and ther mens shaved every day wile them hairy Geeks wuz still eetin raw meet in caves.

The thing to see on Creet we wuz tole wuz yer thurty five hundert yeer old paliss at Knauseous witch is still stand-in morer less. Reezin it is, is cuz wat's left is mostly blow ground. First time I ever see a cassel without no fartifications like walls

*Yer bull werks at knause ous*

or remoats to keep theefs out or slaves in, and no big bad-dlemints fur deefents. All they had to be defensiv wuz jist a cuppla big bull-horns stickin' up like futball goaly posts. Look like a pritty peesabull settup.

Wen we got to that old-time cassel we wuz in a regler heet wave . . . tempachures hire than enny I've ever had even wen I wuz feeverd . . . and yet down in that cassel it wuz cool and breezy, almost as if it wuz air condishun. They had runnin wotter too, and a sistern wat flushed out wat they call here yer nite soils. And we seen a three thousand yeer old ate-teen carrot gold bath-tub.

I started wonderin off all by meself thru the hallwaze of that place. I wuz in sitch a maze that I got soon lost. The wife sed no wunder, that's wat yer sposed to do, cuz this paliss is reely a LabRinse. Knossus wuz the home of yer Minnytory, the bull-hedded sun of yer Creetking hoo wanted peeple to loose ther way in his big house so he cud have them fer supper. Not as gests, but as yer blooplait speshul.

And wen that Creet bunch tocks about bull-hedded they means it litterly. If ya think all this sounds mostly bull, that's wat Creet histry is all about. Insted of bean bull-fiters like yer

Spainish Tory-adorers with ther caips and sords and micky-mouse hats, these Creeters wuz bull-warshippers. Insted of stickin them beests with sords they faced ther buls hed-on and wen he charge, they'd take yer bull by the horns, and leep onto his back with a summersalt. (Ackshully, givin how tricky it wuz, the Creetins therselfs never dun this, they got forners to do it, mostly hostidges frum Grease.)

Theeses, sunuva king of Athins, wuz wun of these. He volunteer to go Creetwords as a Roil sackerfice along with uther yung vicktims. But the mith sez that Theeses beet yer Minnytore by gettin the King's dodder in luv with him, and she balled him a huge hunka string so's he cood find his way outa yer Lavrinth. (I found my way out by yellin my hed off.) The trooth of the story probly is that Theeses excaped wen a big erfquake hit Creet, cozzing a rappid deekline and fallout witch split up ther hole civilly-ization. And I meen big—mebby 9 or 10 on yer Rictum scails.

But yuh cant take away frum Creet that these peeples had air condishning and flush tilets and gold bathtubs thurty five hundert yeer ago. Ther's fokes round our parts in Northren Ontaryio don't have enny of them things yet. And we has the nerf to call these peeple Creetins!!!

# Kyro

Afore we left Parry Sound fer parts unoan, Valeda had tole our fambly dockter her gratest dreem wuz to see yer Sfinks, ever sints she had join a Peer Amid Club back in her erly fiftys. His face went all pail and he tole her she better see a speshulist. She thot he ment a sick-eye-a-tryst, and she got her dandruff up, but he ment a fella hoo gits yuh shot fer topical deceases.

Our travvle agint found us wun down to Trawna and we got along jist fine with him until his neadles cum out. Wen Valeda seen the size of his sick-shooter she pert neer feint. Meself, I thot I had bin used to bein' needled and shafted, but I'd never bin stick it to like that.

This dockter had bin to yer midleest and spent sum time in Eejippt, ware he had even bin a Kyro-practisser, and he sez yuh dassn't go ther without a lotta pree-coshins. Don't drink no water lesson it's boddled, don't eet no sallids or fresh frut, and don't bye nuthin' in the street fer to put in yer mouth. And fer gawd's sake if yiz wants to cum back alive, roll up yer shurtsleave and don't skip these jabs fer titty-nuss, tyfooz, and mull-aria.

Well sir, I gess it all took, cuz weer back home safein Parry Sound. That topical dockter put the shots to us but he never preepair us fer the sites we wuz about to see wen we hit Eejipshun customs with our Veezys in our hand. (Oh yes, ya gotta have wun of them to git in and outa the country, cost ya neer thurty dollar per Veesa, and yer Masterscharger won't do.) Not that them Jippshuns wuzn't extry plite to us, and change our munny into pound after pound of thairs. Mind you, tock about yer filthy luker, sum of their currantsee is reely dirty munny, and limper than me after the thrashing.

But the customs I meen is the way sum peeples dress in this topical country. Wading outside the cussdoms wuz a buncha lokels, and haff of them wuz dress in ther nite-shirts, (bare nooses) with dishycloths on ther heds look like they work fer yer Peeza Huts. Everybuddy wuz bear in the feet sept fer a pare of scandals. Yooda thunk frum the way they looked that they'd slep in that mornin and didden hav time to git dress.

We got a limmuzeen fer to take us to yer Ramadan Inn. (Sorry. I think I got it kinda rong. It wuz yer Ramsey Hillton. Ramadan is yer Arb Eester.) Kyro got more inhibitants than enny sitty in the wirld, give or take Maxyco. Upperds of fifteen millyun soles livs in the wun place, and wen yuh count in the computers that cums in frum all yer sluberbs, yer tocking mebby twenny millyun on enny give-in day. 90 purr-sent of Kyro peeple wuzn't born ther, they cum frum small villedges but wuz too blaim shaimed fer to admitt it!

This wuz eevning resh hour and ther wuz a bumper to bumper crop on the rodes, and nobuddy seem to pay enny ten-shun to redlites. Mebby it's cuz they cant see them on accounta

the smug that seemed well hung all over the sitty. The lacka
vizzlebility maid Valeda nervuss, she felt she wuz in the middel of wun of them Alfy Hitchyercock moovys.

Neveryerless, we wuz delivver alive at our huttel, witch
look pritty much like yer Tronto Hillton or yer Radish-on or yer
Fore Seezin. They pit us up in a room ate-teen flores offa the
ground, witch give us a panick-rammick vue of Kyro. This maid
Valeda even more nervuss, speshully wen she looked down and
out the winder and seen all the rubbel frum ther last urfquake
a cuppla yeer ago, witch register pritty high on yer Rectum
scails. The garbitch and the rubels frum it wuz still thair on the
tops of ruffs, jist abuv ware the londry hung down frum everybuddy's winders. The wife started to shake with her epic der-
mis, and tocked about us gittin in on the ground flore insted.

Meentimes I'm lookin' up our travvle insurients to see if
it incloods enny sitch acts frum God. But Valeda is nuthin if
not artistickle, and she cammed down considerbull wen she
seen afar off them Peer Amids sittin in the sonset witch wuz
settlin slowly in that urbane smawg, all pink 'n purpull.

I wuz still feelin tooristy and wanted to step out into yer
Kyro nitelife, witch wuz oney a cuppla blox away. It wuz called
yer Corneesh, but we never seen a hen in site. Lotsa uther
eetabulls tho'. Kyro is fulla streetvenders, and they must be
poplar, cuz a lotta streetwockers wuz makin out with them
instedda goin home fer supper. They got carts fulla beens,
sweet taters, mangle juice, and sumthin I don't wanna noe
about call cooze-cooze. It's a gud thing we had areddy et cuz I
mite hav bin temt to try it, altho' that topical dockter back
home clames the mane things cums offa those carts is dire-reer
and hippytite-ass.

It wuz Fryday nite, date nite in Canda, but it look to us
more like Nooyeerseeve in Time Squair wen they're wading
fer ther balls to drop. Every car wuz so blaim horny. They don't
blair long like Nooyork, but short and sharp, like to give ya
peerced eers. The drivers never stop fer nuthin' and it wuz

wirth yer life as a pederastrian crossin the streets. But we never felt no dainger, as long as we staid on the sidewocks.

Everybuddy look at us plezzant and most of them spoke Anglish. Sum of them streetwockers went out of ther way to welcum us. A few sed they had relations in Muntry All or Edmington, they wernt shure witch. Wun fella sed his wife wuz jist crazy about sumthing on the Kyro TV called "Annagreen Gaybars."

Sum even invited us to stay with them instedda of us puttin up with yer RamSeas Hiltin. They also hoped they cood stay with us wen they cum to Canda, and finisht up by taken us to ther dorestep and tryin to sell us Arbick Poorfumes. Valeda haggel with them usin' the saim teckneeks she had develupp at the Flee Markit every Thursdy in Elmvale, southa Parry Sound, wile I wuz buyin' pigs. She haggel well too, witch put them streetsellars in transparts of delite, as if they didden want her to seddle on the furst price. They kep sayin "No charge to look, no charge to look!!" but the wiffs offa them poor-fumes wuz too musky fer her, so she end up insted byin' sum anteeky lookin liddle statyew of a Faro-ess hoose naim wuz print on the back: "Maiden TaiWan."

Back in our rum on that ate-teenth flore, the noise seamed jist as much as wen we wuz back on the streats. We close the winders but that catter-walling kep on all nite. Valeda reedin frum the gidebook sed Our Lord Jeezis spoke his furst wurds in Kyro, but I dout if anybuddy herd them.

# Old Geezer

Urly, if not brite, we wuz coamed and curried, so we lobbied ourselfs downstares to meet Assya, a universally granulate hoo wuz gonna take us over to yer Peer Amid and then round the town to a cuppla Muslin Mosks, wun of witch wuz start up by Moe Hamid Ah Lee! (Cash Yiz Clay that wuz.)

Yer Peer Amid and yer Sfinks is on the outerskurts of a town called Geezer, witch is acrost wat Assya called Denial. She sed it's the biggest, longist rivver in the wirld, and I wunderd wat she wuz tocking about, but Valeeda noo. She hit the Nile rite on the hed. It wuz jist as brown as yer Bloo Dan Yube, but I herd the Nile wuz called Bloo too, and even Wite in sum of its upper parts, but whadda ya expeck after a jurny thousins of miles thru all that brown sand?

Old Geezer is reely a sublurb of Kyro, and so is Memfis. Valeda thot mebby we shood stay over a extry day and take in Graceyland, but nobuddy frum yer Tooryist bored seam to noe ware it wuz. Geezer is closern Memfiss, and fulla life erly in the mornin, with a lotta peeple in durbins and niteshirts (witch our gide Assya called golabbyiz) and the odd cammel. We finely got outa town and into yer Sarah dessert, and stop outside a big pile of rox. Wen Valeda ast our girl gide why we wuz stoppin in sitch a dessolit place, Assya sed "This is yer Grate Peer Amid of Cheeps."

We got out and look up at this man-maid mounting bilt of tuns of stones . . . eech of them at leest cuppla tuns hevvy. Ther's two and a haff millyun of them all pile up on toppa eech uther. Assya sed ther use to be Seven Wunders of yer Wirld, and this is the oney wun left. Tock about yer Roaling Stones, nobuddy got any idear how they got their piles like that, but they wuz set in plaice mebby seven thou yeers back. The theery is they use sum kind of leavers. My own theery is all them rocks wuz uplifted before the Law of Gravelty wuz passed. However they dun it, we mussin ignoar the fack that it wuz bilt with the swett of man's kine.

I wuz kinda dissapoint that the top wuzn't pointy and all shiney like it is on yer Yank doller bill. Valeeda wuz sprized that it wernt all smoothin'eeven, but our gide Assya tole her that it started out cuvvered in Polish limestoan. It shon in the sun like a lectric lite, but wuz strip of all that by Arbs twelf hunnert yeer ago fer to bild ther mosks. To them as warship Alley, this pile wuz jist a conveenience stoan quorry.

Wun of them niteshurt fellahs (that's wat farmers is call in Eejippt, fellahs) appeer outa nowares and ast us if we wanted to accumpaninny him to the toppa the peermid fer twenny pounds. Valeda figgerd she'd lose morn twenny pounds if she tride it, and wornd me agin havin a cornary thrombone-sis. I thot it wuz along way to go fer to ern twenny pounds, but the niteshurt fella ment I shood pay him, not the vicey of yer versy. Assya maid the suggestiv that we go inside insted, sints it wuz illeagle to git up on yer rocks.

So we went below on yer Cheeps insted, down in his depps, fer to see ware the old fella wuz burried. Put me in mind of bein back in Subbery wen we went down on a mind shaft. Ya hadda be bent dubble heer too, and I don't reckamendit if yer wun of them cluster-foabs. Besides, wen ya git down in the bowls of it, ther's not a durn thing to see . . . jist a emty basemint. Valeda had herd about all them graiv rubbers, how they wood strip enny Faero handy of all his blongings, but Assya sez mosta the stuff is back in Kyro at the guvmint Mewseemen, witch lader we wood be took in by.

Ther's sposed to be sumthing magicle under these try-angled piles accorn to a artickle I red in yer Breeder's Diejist. Like I kep wishin' I had brung sum raizer blaids along cuz the affluence of yer peeramid is sposed to them git even more sharp. Valeda wunderd about enny of them old Faros having the curse.

Our gide girl, Assya, hoo is a traned experk on all ded things, sez that them cursus wuz jist to friten away toom robbers. Ther wuz a graivyard open up last munth witch had corpsus of uppern middel class offishuls frum five thou yeers ago. These wuz the shrivel serpints that had help orgynize the bildin of yer Cheep Peeramid. And ther oan liddler toom had the

Sfinks
with
Shriner

curse on it witch sed "Cum in heer and lines, crockydiles and hippy-optimists will git yiz."

I had brang along my old Shriner hat frum our Randy-Gar Mistycal Grottoe back home, and Valeda brung along her Browny. I wuz determin to git took betwean the lyin's pause of that big Sfink statchel with the enemma-mattic smile. Valeda wuz all set to flash wen we wuz tole we cooden git that close or we wood git in deep doodoo frum them as is in charge of yer hole Sfinker operayshin. So we back off and rent-a-Cammel insted. Tuck me a wile to git over the hump on that cammel, and she shure is a sprize wen she rizes arsend first. If yiz don't leen back with a 45 degree angel, yer libel to end up grounded.

After that we wuz back acrost the river (Correckshun: The River) and visit that Cashyus Clay mosk I tole yiz about. Oney it ain't name after the same hevvywate champeen bocksir you and I mind—flotes like a bea, stings like a flutterby. This Moe Hammits Alee wuz a Turker frum I-standbull hoo wuz deetermin to bring Eejippt into yer nineteen senchry, witch wuz wat they wuz in at the time, and most of them still is.

We tuck off our shooze so we wooden durty up them

carpits, but we didden have to git down to preying on our hansa-neeze or slaaming arselfs, jist look around and keep our mouths shut up. Valeda wunderd if they filled this minny-skydoam like we don't do with our cherch back hoam. Asya sed ther has bin a Fuddled Mentalist reevival, but she shutter a bit as she sed so, cuz it's bin bad fer tooryism witch is her bred-in budder. She herself wuz a Cop-Tick, witch don't meen she's on the pleece farce, but a Eejippt Krisstyun, of witch we didn't reelize ther wuz enny. (In fack, yer curnt Sexaterry Genial of our Untied Nayshins, Booterass Booterass Golly, is wun of yer Copts.)

Wun in ten Eejippters is Jeeziz fans, and that makes them the biggest minner-ority in the land. But yule never heer our Bibel vergin in enny Eejippt histry. They got no reckerd of Hebrooze ever bin enslave heer. The book of Exxitdust to Eejippt histerians is nuthin but friction, and the oney person ever had Jews bild Peer Amids wuz Yule Brimmer under the direckshun of Sessle Bee Duh Mill. And ther's no menshun heer of that Sharlatan Hesstin neether.

Them Eejippters had anuther histerical peeriod they don't menshun, way back about sexteen hunnert B.B.C. Fer 108 yeers they wuz rool over by furners called HickSoss. They cum frum summers in Azure and they beet the nickers offa the hoam-groan armys cuz they had two things the lokels dint have and had never seen before—horses and weels—witch put together makes yer charryet. You'd think the bunch that log-rolled all them yuge stones into a peer-amid wooda gon the nex step and invent the weel, but nosirree. Kyro peeple still don't wanna tock about it.

Alluva suddint on our way to summers elts, we wuz passin a big semmatairy that had a lotta Teevee Airials. We wunderd if sum Faro had bin burried thair and had the cable put in fer his post-mortis cumfurts. Nossireebob, them Teevys wuz fer the live ones. This semetairy wuz call yer Sitty of the Ded, yet hunderds of inhibitants wuz ressadint thair. They even got busstops tween the tooms! They shud call it yer Lastmile-but-

one. Them mozzeleeums is a poplar adress on accounta the
Kyro housin shortedge, which is coz by the fack that 95
preesent of yer popillation of Eejippt lives on 5% of yer lands,
and every ten munths the copulation is increese by a millyun
more poor soles.

The rent fer livin amung yer ded is steep, not cheep. This
has bin goin on sints yer 19-twennys, and rent controled (like
us back in Endeepee Ontaryo) so that them landlards that owns
this big Necker-oppolus don't bother fixin up the rooms tween
the tooms. The ded gits more care than yer livin. Semmatairy
visiters cums regler and visits ther ded amid the live wuns, and
sum of them tooms is rite inside the livid-in houses. Valeda ast
wat ya do with a toom rite in the middel of yer dwell-in?
Assyuh sed the liv-ins probly use it as ther dine-in room tabel,
with flours pervided regler by yer deseased's intimit relayshins.

Speekin of yer deer deeparted, we endid up our long day's
Kyro jurny at this coalossus of a guvmint museemen that had
horded up mosta the gud things that's now missin frum all
them old Faeryo's tooms. I wanna tell yuh them Theevs missed
a lot, and so will yew if yuh never gits to see the post-mortal
lewt that that mewseeum got instore fer yuh. They got more
mummys than a day-cair senter at close-in time.

Summa them mummys got bewdiful chests wat they bin
lade in, but the best of them all is yer trezzures of yer Toot
Uncommon. This teenyager (the kid wuza oney 19 wen he
kickoff) got more crown jools than he kin shake his stick at,
and two goaled statutes of hisself pluss a cuppla throans and
three beers to git burried in, pluss four minnycher cawfins jist
fer to holed up his intrails!

And he never got evaded by enny of them engraved rubbers. Valeda thot it wuz the most bewdyful funeereal parler
she'd ever bin in, and I figgerd that this poor thurd wirld country we wuz visitin cood pay off ther nashnul dett if they jist
soled off the chattles of ther nashnul ded.

# Up Yer Asswan to Abby Simpel

We hadda git up at three a'cluck this mornin' fer to catch the plain that wuz takin' us all the way to see the big faros down at Abby Simpel. Valeda had to be tocked hard into gittin all up in the air agin, but it wuz the oney way to git down ther close by yer Soo Dan witch is wair them big statutes wuz.

Wun way in witch ainshint Eejippt wuz like pree-Conflagellation Canda is that it wuz divide into Upper and Lower. This don't meen French and Anglish like us, but South and North. We had jist bin Lower in Kyro, and now we wuz a bout to be on ther Uppers.

We wuz bust lickadee splits to the Eejipptair airport at fore aclock in the mornin, and at that time it didden seem to madder about goin thru all them redlites. But wen we gits to our neckstop, yer airport, everything goze at yer mail's pace. Wun thing ya shood lern about tooryism, it's allways hurry up and wate. The plain cum inta vue about two hour lader, look like a crap duster to me, all propped insted of jetted. Reeminded Valeda of her first flite and she started to git the wind up, so I slip a Grav-all pill in her Sevenupps.

This plain wuz pack to the gunnils till we reeched Asswan, ware haff of them tooryists got off, wile the resta us geered arselfs up fer them Abby Simbel life-stiles. Reedin up about it in yer gidebook on the way, I reelize that our hole expedishun wuz to see sumthin' that had bin faiked. These big statchures never got carv up wair we wuz gonna see them, on accounta they had bin remoove to make rum fer Laik Nassir, witch wuz cremated by the penned-up wotters of yer Asswun Dam. Sints the laik wuz naim after the nashnulist Prime Minster hoo got the last king of Eejippt Fruck off his throan, I figgerd the dam to hav bin injuneered by Nassir, that's his baby. Terns out the hole dam thing wuz bilt by Serviet injuneers frum Ma's Cow. The pint of all this deeconstructivness wuz to help Eejippt aggerculcher. But it hazzint. Not by a damsite: prennial earigation has brung prenniel earatation. Ther poor farmers jist cum thru ate leen yeers with not much of that black loamy silt gittin all the way up yer Delter hard by Alec Sandra like it useter. Sum rivver foke has to eet yer pap-iris plants fer to stay alive. Oh they do git morn wun crap a yeer, mebby two or three, but by pushin up yer wotter tabel, yer dose a salts haz been increse, witch is gonna rejuice yer yeelds and make furtle land eevenchilly barn. And all this controle fludding seams to do is to grow more weed in yer wotter, witch eether has to be cleen out by hands, or pizened out with pestysides. (Gess witch they use? ha ha) Not to menshun Bill Harzia* . . . witch is a vire-ass coz by liddle orgasms in the dam wotter.

This heer projeck also maid homeliss a hunnert thousand Nooby-Uns livin heer jist north of yer Sedan. The Kyro guvmint bilt them sum concreet blockhouses thurty yeer ago witch preestressed them even more, cuz ther new hoams look to them like tooms. Too bad they didden reelowcade all them semmutairy Kyro peeple insted!

*Bilharzia
Ed.

The oney reel attenshun give to creecher cumfurts in this aria wuz pade to them ded Faros and ther Faresses, and this mite not a happen eether if it hadden bin fer the culcher part of yer Untidy Nations, UNISEXCO.

But nobuddy wuz thinkin about sitch things wen we deplained at Abby Simpel, witch is not reely a town or even a villedge, but jist a cleckshun of frantical sooveneer sellers pushin ther wairs in yer face. We excape wen they bust us over to Lake Nassir, witch look fer all the wirld like Lake Cooch Itching or yer Gorgin Bay hard by yer Wasaggy Beeches. It wuz a brite sunny day, witch seems reedumdum to me now, cuz that's all yuh ever gits in Eejippt. (Yer avridge ranefall goze frum nill to zeero.)

Yuh don't git to see them monstird statures rite at furst. Ther's a liddle mounting (reely a plat-toe) blockin yer vue. But alluva suddin ya terns the corner and gits yer breth took away. Valeda sed it put her in mind of Mount Rushymore with them Yank heds of stait oney heer they do up the hole boddy. Heer's a buncha them old time roolers and ther wimmenfoke all stoned and sittin in frunt of yuh a hunnerd foot hy. They got ther liddle kids by ther sides mebby oney ten foot eech. (Kids in them days wuz cut down to size and noo ther plaice.)

Wun statchel is of Ray, yer sungod, with a spaid beerd and wat look like a big bowlin pin on toppa his hed. Nex to this Gawd sat Faro Ramsey and his wife. I dunno why they named a contraseptor after old Ramsey hoo rool 55 wives fer 67 yeer and had morn 200 kids to speek of, but Valeda sed mebby it's to be on yer safe's side. Praps Eejippt is becumming anuther condom nation. I thot ther wuz more kids abuv Ramsey on yer freeze up toppa the tempel, but they tern out to be sakerd Baaboons.

The saim thot occur to me heer as wen I saw yer Peer Amid. How do them Eejippters do it? How did they git ther blocks off frum ware they wuz to heer? I meen yer modrens, not yer old-timers. Cuz they hadda chop up all them statutes into seprit blox like so much cheez, and then ree-assa-semble them hire up on land ware it's allways dry. I dunno witch is the more amazin feets, moovin all this rig a few yeers ago, or bildin all of it in the furst place.

Ile give yiz a frinstants. They had the inside of this tempel rigged up with statutes too. And they set them so that wen the sun cum into yer hippystile hall (this is yer inner tempel held up by big colyums, not a buncha sextys peeple in Nayroo jackits and belly bottem jeens) it hit on three of yer fore deeatitties inside. This incloods yer sungod and a cuppla uther deetys, but them archytex had it so rigged that yer sunlite don't hit on yer

Mr and Miz
Faro,
Ejipshun
Gothic

Mistress of the Nite. They delivveratly missus that Nut, the gawdass of Nite, so she kin be kep in the dark! And them raze strikes exackly at the twenny furst of Febyouairy and Ocktober. But mark ye, wen they move this tempel 200 yard back and sexty foot hire a cuppla millenemas lader, that saim sun cums in that innard Sankatum on yer twenty-secund insted yeer twenny furst. Close enuff fer a seegar!

# Up Denial!

Wen we flu back up to yer Asswan aerport every offishul there look at us kinda grimm. They have a speshul farce of Torst Antickwitty Pleece (that's wat ther called) and they had called on the Eejippt army to brake into a Muslin mosk and wipe out seven fuddlementalists. I ast sumbuddy hoo wuz jist leevin on our plain back to Kyro, why the pleece wood wanta nock off peeple durin ther cherch serfusses. He glair at me and sed: "It were a case a sulfa defents, cuz them fannyticks wuz arm to the tooth with ham grenaids!!"

These Muslins got a strong follying, make no mistaik,

speshully after that big erfquaik wen the guvmint didden giv much help and these ex-streamists cum forth with blankits and fud and all kinds of aids. Valeeda wuz on her nerfs enuff jist havin bin on a plain agin, but wen she herd that we mite be runnin into terrier-asts on the ground, I tole her we shud hed fer the river. We had alreddy booked ourselfs on a croose of Denile, so I grab a taxi fer to git to our Nilebote and git a flote before the resta the passinjers grabbed all the outside cabbings.

We needen have reshed. Ther wuz 2 rivverbotes docked side by side, naimed after the top teenaage gawds of Eejippt, *Ices* and *O Sire Us,* and neether wun wuz a-crawlin with lifes. Terns out that our ship, yer Ices, had a croo of 78 and a passinjer list of elevens.

Our nine fella tooryists wuz mostly Amerkens workin in yer Midleest. Terns out we wuz all pritty compaddabull, incloodin' the croo on our crooze, hoo cooden do enuff fer us, on accounta ther wernt enuff of us fer them to do much fur.

Valeeda wuz hopin' we could flea rite up yer Nile, away frum enny trubble but our gide hoo had jist cum on bored sed ther wuz too much to see hear-a-bouts. His naim wuz Andray, a Eejippshun hoo had bin eddicated at a French Universally, and he wuz purfickly try-languid. He sed that the pleece ackshun in that Ass-one mosk shood skeer off them hostel Muslins fer quite sum time. Furst place he wanted to show us wuz anuther Muslin mosk!

This one wuz more of a ded issyuh, sints it's a one-man bildin and contanes oney the remanes of Aggie Kan. I mind him as the fella use to sit on his scails and git his wate in dymonds and platten'um for his berfdy present. He wuz frum Packystand, but he use to winter heer fur his roomatizzy arthurite-us at the saim hoetell, yer Catter Act, wair Aghasta Christy writ about *Death on Denial.* Aggie's missus, yer Baygum Can, cums heer fer about fore munths a yeer and jist stairs acrost the rivver at her man. She has deranged to have every daya the yeer a fresh roze on his beer.

To go passed old Aggie's mozzeleeum we hadda git off our big ship and take a liddle krafft witch has bin use on this water fer thousans of yeers. It's called a Flucker, the muther of all sale-botes. Valeda, bean a Martime bloonozer, tuck to yer Flucker like a duck, and wuz soon swingin with ther boom as parta the croo.

We first swung round Kitchyner Eyeland ware that old Impeeriuss Briddish Feeld-Marshul of the saim naim had hisself a botenny garding. It wuz fulla eggsottick plants like Roil pams with wite trunks, old narled sickamoors, and accasian trees with leefs like a Sultana's beerd. Ther wuz a surprize buncha bloomers . . . redden wite hawlyhox! . . . jist to make Valeda feel homely fur her flour plot back home in Parry Hoot. It wuz like findin our Canajun flag in fornparts. We finish off this liddle trip by mooving past Ella Fanteen Eyeland, so-call cuz the grayrox all round the bottom of it looks like the tale-end of big packy-dermissus.

Tooryism in Eejippt meens sooveneers, and we wuz plaiged everywares by sailsmen, on shore, on wotter, even IN wotter. They even follied us back to our big ship, yer Ices, and stud on the dox and throo garmints up at the wimmin on bored. All three of our wimmin riz to the bate, and enjoid havin' a reel hag-haggle . . . harem-scarem pants and rinestone stummickers got throan on the ship and back onshore, then back ondex. Sum of them yung lads cooda pitch fer yer Bloojays or Exposers.

But it wuz them gals of ours as scored and beet them on dock wen it cum to bargin-inning, and they all end up with Arb costooms fulla seequintses. That nite afer dinndinns, (that's wat wun of our passinjers called it . . . sounds to me like a old Arb wurd) we had a Impromtwo party. The wimmin dress up in ther hoory (that's wat they're called!) outfits, and the resta us dun wat we cood to git into the rite spearits. I dress up as a mummy usin' a role of tilet paper, and it wuz Valeda dun the

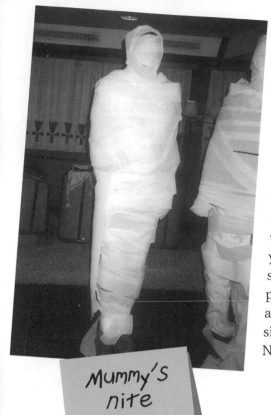

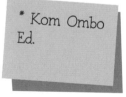

Mummy's nite out

rap job. The croo join in with potsenpans and a cuppla floots and a reel drum. Frum then on we wuz all frends, despike enny fuddled mental thretts. Them crooboys plaid fer us wile we orgynized arselfs into a congy line. Then the croo tot us all how to billydants, and you shooda seen my Valeda shaken hur epicdermist and puttin' moovemints before the ass-embly that I hadden seen sints our hunnymoon in Nagger Falls!

# Rite Between Yer Tempels

Wen we reganed conshy-enshusness nex mornin we wuz alreddy dock at a old tempel, Kum On Bo.*

This partickler tempel is deddicate to a god hoo wuz reely a crocky-dial with a man's boddy. Them old time Eejippsies thunk of them ugly beest as absolootly deevine, and they even had sum crock mummys still lyin around witch give Valeeda chivvers uppendown her cocksix (witch is the bottom of yer spine, so no smart

* Kom Ombo Ed.

remarx). To me them allygaited corpusses jist look like bleech-out driffwood.

Ther wuz a obbylisk a hunnert foot long lyin' on its side with a crack up it, witch is why it had never had its ereckshun. I still marvill at how them old-timers cooda dun all that lifting without dubble herny-ating therselfs. But in this wun case, them old fellahs coodn't git it up.

Valeda wuz offal disappoint at the lacka culler in the pitch-ers on the colyums. Andy, our Eejippt gide with the Frenchy ax-sent, sed ther wuz lotsa cullers slapped on wen they first got the brush put to her, but it's the carpin dye-ox-hide ex-hail by all us toorists is wat is now bleeching them out. That's why he tole us wen we wuz inside them roons looking at the old muriels not to "breeze wit your mouse."

Our gide sed Jippshuns luvved brite cullers, and used to paint ther ownselfs up a storm as well as ther bildins. He sez they used coal round ther eyes! It wuz instedda macnamara, witch sounds kinda panefull to me. And not jist the wimmen but the men paint up ther faces too, incloodin lip-rooge bee-tween ther cheaks. Fer the more matchose of yer mas-kalin sects all this musta seam a reel drag.

Still erect
after all
these yeers!

Our bote hedded fer Ed Foo, anuther tempel, altho' it sound to me like a Chinee restrunt. This wun is dessicated to a fulkin-hedded god called Horass. Ther's a pare of them big burds outside the tempel, full lenth in granit about the hite of a baskyball plair. The beedy-ide look on them feerse birds wood make yoo go home and change yer unnerwairs.

This tempel stud aloan with nuthin elts around. Reesin fer that is cuz stone wuz oney use fer tempels, but fer the common peeples they hadda make doo with mud, and ther liddle dwell-ins musta got warsh away, wile yer stone stuck.

They shure maid a fuss about ther Faros in them tempels. My gol, you'da thunk yer avridge rooler wuz the gawd they wuz warshippin. A lotta peeple in histry started to bleeve that, speshully them Faros themselfs, if ya bleeves sum of the tittles they give therselfs wen they got on the throan. Mosta them Jippshun kinks had at leest five tittles. Heer's a sampel . . . "King of Uppernlower Eejippt, Son of a Horus, Mighty Bull, Tall of Fethers, and Two Ladees Man." That's like me callin myself "King Charles Ewart of Metropopolitan Parry Sound, Son of a Farquharson, Mitey of Kilt, and Spreader of Culcher."

The thing wat shock Valeda is that these tempels wuz never fer yer commons peeples. Us torsts wuz let in, cuz we pade our dooze, but back then, it wernt like regler cherch. Oney them preests and faros wuz aloud inside fer to warship the god.

It wuz wen they had a festerall, and brung the god outside to sellabate, did ennybuddy git a glimps. And them gods hadda git out fer a airing wunce in a wile. Like fer exampel, this falkin god had a wife hoo wuz a reel cow, Haw Thorn, with her own tempel uprivver, and she use to cum down fer a visit every sex munths. Sumtimes these mix marges works out.

The soil heer is black like yer Haulin' Marsh back home in Ontaryo, but I never seen a trackter in all them feelds. It's all dunkywork. The crop heerabouts is shuggercain, and after razing all that cain it's ship dreckly onto ralecars frum the backs of yer dunky. Them liddle asses gits so loded yuh kin hardly see them fer wat they're carrion.

Not a pig in site. Figgers. Never seen a chick neether, cum to think of it, jist dux and geeze. Funny lookin wite birds in the feelds called yer Eegrets. Look like a goose on a strick dye-it. Sheeps cums in wuns or tooz, not flocked. Ther's the odd cammel, and a even odder waterd-buffloe witch puts me in mind of eether a shave musscox or a cow with steereo horns.

Every yuman has a cuvverup on top so they won't git stroked by ther sun. Wimmen wares nuthin but black, topp ta toze, eggsept fer them as is yung and singel—they goze fer Daiglo cullers. Oney the men has shooze, wimmin and childern is all bearfut. Wimmin carrys bundels biggern themselfs on ther heds. Eether that or plastical 5 gal contaners. Cant tell wether them wimmen is gittin gas or wotter, and we saw a cuppla yung feemail beetin ther close on the rocks. Valeda sed she expeckted to see a Maytag man beehind them, crine his eyes out.

The houses round heer is wun story, mostly non-descripp with no winders, and maid outa bricks witch wuz maid outa mud. It look like a gud rane wood slooce the place into the ground till it look like choclit moose. But it won't ever happen cuz the wether heer is always dryer than our Speech frum the Droan in the Ottawa House of Comics.

They git all ther wet frum underneeth wen the river ovverruns itself every spring. In frunta the houses they got crummly mud walls with jist stix to hole them together. And yuh cant tell ther house frum ther barn. They got no ruffs eggsept shugger cain stocks throan acrost. Sum has bloo doors, and a cupple has drawrins on ther sidewalls to show that they hav maid the Hodge to Mecker. (Yer Hodge is yer pills-grim-age Allah way to ther Profit's burfplace in Shoddy Arapeyuh.)

Gittin off the buss to ship out on our bote agin we wuz stop by hords of liddle kids beggin us fer . . . not candy or bubbly gum . . . but ballspint pens! Wisht our flash-and-blud Orville had the same thirst fer eddication. He don't even rite pust-cards.

# Ded Vally

Today we stop at Luck Sore, a pritty much Arb town, at leest in yer backstreets wair we druv thru frum the bote in a horse with a buggy beehind. Them liddle narra streets wuz fulla gotes, sum tetherd and uthers free as yer breeze, witch in the case of a gote yuh better not be on the windy side of. This place use to be call Theebs, witch wuz in its own time the Ottawar of Eejippt, a capitall place fer Faros to live. And dye too. The Eest bank wus fer yer live ones, wile yer Westbankers wuz in yer ded zoan.

Seams like them old Eejippsies thot about deth frum the minit they got borned. Wun of the first tecksbooks they had wuz a kind of map of yer nex wirld called a Book of yer Ded, with all kinds of direckshuns on how to git off propper into the last sunset after you've bot the biskit. It tuck seventy daze fer to salt away yer deerly beluvvid into a Mummy and I AIN'T ABOUT TO DEESCRIBE ALL THAT IN CASE YER GONNA HAV LUNCH. (It's mostly a matter of drysalting the boddy like it wuz a fish. Newfunlanders mite still remember a simlar rich-you-all.)

In the old, old pie-in-ear daze ded peeple wuz jist put in yer fatal posishun in a hole in the sand and cuvverd up. But as sassiety got more sofistificated deth becum a race fer to keep up with yer Joanses. A Faro started workin on his toom and the deth mask to go on his sarcoffygust as soon as he assended up on his throan.

But no more Peer Amid clubs. Them interminal tryangles went outa stile cuz they wuz too much of a eezy marker fer toomrobbers. So these old Theebins started hidin' ther roil cor-pusses amung yer Hard Rock. That's wat we had cum to see in this Vally of yer Kinks, Queans and Nobels. Tut's toom is heer with his boddy still inside it, but it wernt open fer bizness that day.

This hole landescape is absolootly nuthin' to look at, eggsept fer a pointy mountin up top witch looks like a manmaid peeramid, but it's all Muther Naycher. You'd think this place wuz a uninhibited willderness if you didden noe wat wuz undyground. I dunno how they conduckted them toom drillsessyuns thru that rock, but they dun a master toolin-dye job job. Our moddren hi-tex wood be hard putt to cum up with as good . . . tunnels five hundert foot long and strait as my sexlife. Valeda thot ther hired hands musta bin pritty overwork, espeshully wen they wuz always in heet by the swett of ther browse, but our gide sed they had a regler ate hour day jist like sitty peeple still has. Fore ours afore nockin off fer lunch and fore ours after. They even had a sit-me-down strike wunce wen they didden git ther lunch! And they allways had a napp after, jist like I do on the farm.

With all the pree-coshins of hidin' away ther ded, it didden help enny of them mummy heer frum gittin ramsacked (eggsept fer yung Toot hoo helled off til 1922). This ramsacking genrully tuck place wen times wuz hard, and pore peeple got more consern about this wirld than gittin sum old king reddy fer the next. Most of them toom robbings musta bin inside jobs. Our gide figgers the gards and the preests mite a clabrated on them smashin grab-operayshins.

Ther's no artyfishul eclectric lites down ther, so the gide stays outside the toom with a meera witch reflecks well on us. Cuz we kin pass the lite on usin a peece of Polish mettle. The oldtimers used linnin, so our gide tride it with a Kleenecks. Didden work.

Wen we cum out into yer brite sunlite we run into a groop of yung Canajun bagpackers hoo had bin roamin the wirld fer haff a yeer and didden noe nuthin about wat wuz goin on back hoam. I dint have the hart to tell them Not Much, speshully fer Canajuns as yung as they wuz, so I jist smile and tock about the wether. Here, not our winter back home, witch sounded as gawd-offal as our econmee.

Them yung Canuckers tole us to be sure to see the paliss of Eejippt's only femail Faro, Quean Hadshutshop. She wuz jist over the hill, this old Quean, so we went, having bin goosed by them bagpaggers to give her a gander. We wuzn't sorry. Her tempel-toom is the most modren of all the old time piles we ever seen. Even more modren than mosta our contempuary bildins back home, on accounta it's hevvily ramped and compleetly weelchare assessibull!

So this wuz a woeman wella hed of her time. In fack, tho' them Eejipshuns cum mutch erlier than yer Greaks, they wuz a long ways ahed in ther femmynist treetmint of wimmen. These Eejipt femails cud own ther own propitty, and sumtimes a fellah cud becum Faro, not becuz of hoo he wuz, but only cuz he got married to a ded Faro's dotter. Nun of yer secund class citizenry heer, speshully with Cleopatterer and Hatshupshet.

This Quean married her own bruther (famlys shure stuck together in them daze) but he pass on before enny child-baring, and instedda lettin her hazbin's kid bruther take over, she shunt him aside, give herself the job, and put on hurself a fake beerd. She dun good roolin' too, speshully with forners affairs in the land of Punt. She whip up a lotta traid with them Punters, exchangin her herb and spicers fer a cuppla their Jyraffs and uther exostic aminals.

That cast-asside kid bruther, Th'Utmost, got his revench after his sisternlaw went west fur gud. He deeface her statchures and hack her naim outa any menshun of her on bildins and monnymints.

We went on to Denderer, hoam of yer Goddass Hawthorn, the deety in charge of luvvin mewsick. Ya mind she's the cow goddass got married up with that bird Horace, the hock faced god with the beedy eye and the sharp beek. Hawthorn's pile

weelchare
accessibull
in 1400 BBC

of a shrine sits all by itself in the middel of the Sahairy. After
yuh gits past the mudwall out frunt, yer facing the Grate Haul
of Colyums, and on top of eech is the womanly face of
Hawthorn, 'xcept those cow eers make her look like that Dr.
Spock on yer old TV Star Dreck. A lot of her faces has bin
deefaced, cuz this tempel got tern lader into a Cop Tick
Cherch, and her imedges got scratched, and them Cop con-
vurts hacked out a lotta them wall paintins too. I spose these
Christyun vandles thot this wood git them into Hevven, jist
like them Eejipshuns thot carvin these statchels up in the furst
place wood git them eeterminal life.

　　We busstopped in Abby Dose, a big infurmry fer ded Faros
and ther rellicks, kinda like yer Middlin Martered Shriners. It
wuz turble hot. They keep sayin' it aint yer heet, it's yer
humannity, so I bot a fan maid outa brite cullerd wull fer wun
Eejippt pound. Valeda thot I shooda bot a fly wisk insted cuz
weer surround by them pesky creechers, small but bothersum.
No wunder all them Faros holds a flail in ther hand as well as
a crook. They makes dandy fly-swotters.

# Lucksore and Weery

I'm still a bit dizzy frum all this culcher, and am startin to
throb a bit between the tempels. I had wore my niteshirt and
Pizza hut durbin cuz it were so hot in that King Vally, but it
aint so hot in them rocky tooms, so to-day I had yer sniffuls
and a slite case of yer green appel quickstep. But our gide tole
us we hadda git up erly and go thru both Lucksore and Carnack
cuz they wuz the biggest rooned bildins weel ever git to see
this side of yer Canary's Worf.

They aint jist the work of wun liddle Faro but the reesult
of 2,000 yeers of a buncha Faros tryna topp eech uther with
ther pursnal monyoumints.

Furst thing ya see in Lucksore is a Avenyoo road of Sfinkses,
90 members of this lion's club, but all with the face of a Ram
in frunt! Them sheepish hedded Sfinkses use to stretch two and
a haff killermeeters all the way to the tuther tempel at
Carmack, with nary a ewe turn. I didden feel like that much
of a wock, but Valeda wuz full of the old jinicker. She went rite
up to wun of them deckerated tellyfone poles they call
obbylisks to look at the pitchers on it, but she cooden make
heds er tales. Our gide tole us it wuz a lotta poppygander about
that Yule Brimmer Faro, Ramsey Too, winnin a big baddle with
the Hit Tites, wen ackshully the frackass wuz a draw.

This obblisc is twice as hy as yer Bellpoles back home. Ther
had bin anuther obbylisk heer too, but she end up in Parse,
Frans, dreckting traffic round yer Plotz Della Concurd. (The
same wun Valeda and I clang to fer deerlife as the French trafficking rored around us.) They musta export a hole buncha
these big pointy things, cuz ther's wun hard by yer Tems in
Lunnon, Angland called Cleopatterer Sneedle, and anuther in
Roam neer yer Fattycan.

By swinjer if that gide of ours didden wock us them two

and a haff killyermeeters over to that uther tempel, yer Car Nack, and Valeda went haply along with him, cuz she use to heer a lot about Car-knack on yer Laid Laid show with John E. Carson.

Oh my gol wen I got to them Carnackers did I ever feel small lookin' up at them pillers that's holdin things up fur that tempel. They sure thunk big, them oldtimers. This yuge sucker of a place of warship is 1,220 footlong and 338 wide. Inside these colyums yuh cood hide Sin Palls, Sin Peeter and Noted Dames and still hav rum leftover fer yer Moron Tabbynackers. Lots more coal-ossle statchels of that Ramsey yer Secund here, up to sexty foot hy. He musta had a feeriorty complecks to be so insect-cured. His wife gits a bit of a look in: on his biggest statute yuh kin see the liddle woman between his laigs. She cums about up to his neeze. Valeda thinks that's about parr fer the corse even now.

Nobuddy eggsept us toorists is follying uppendown the Nile after them Faros these days. Eejipshuns reely havn't dun that fer a duzzen hunnert yeers becuz that's wen that profit Moe Hammid tern mosta them into Muslins. A lotta these old-time tempels has bin tern into mosks. Ther wuz times wen we had to git outa the roons so them troo belevers cood hav ther midday prair meetin. That's wen they all bowse down and faces Mecker.

The daze and daze of all this seein the sites put me to thinkin. All the gilt and culcher of them long ago Faros wuz maid possabull by aggerculcher. The thing that aint change frum time in memoriam is yer fellahs that still tills the soil. And that soil is still fertly-ized the saim way it wuz five thou yeer ago. Fludd wotters. Wat maid Eejippt ritch wuz the fack that they had sirpluss grain wen everybuddy round them wuz starvin. And they dun all this back then without havin to prey fer rane, lik the resta yer Middeleest! If they got too liddle or too much water, Eejipshuns allways had enuff sirpluss in storge fer to ride over wat they calls yer hyeena yeers. (They don't menshun it wuz a Hebrood naim Joesiff with his coded menny cullers hoo give them the ideer of storin' up wen yer fat and goin on wellfare wen yer leen.)

Them Faros acknowledge ther dett by deranging to hav farm wirk continyew after deth. On sum of them carved up toom walls they got pitchers of Faros wirkin ther own hevvinly feelds. Sure, sure! Ile betcha my shurt them crown heds never dun a lick, but they wuz smart enuff to hav took along into ther tooms a lotta little dolls dress up like farmers to do the reel afterlife work. It wuz farmers, not faros, that maid Eejippt prosper, and doan chew fergit it.

Most happy fellah

# Post-Ambull

*Yo Orville! By the time ya gits this weel be home in yer face and checkin up on all the chores yer sposed to have dun! Yer muther is reely flyin~ I meen in a plain wat goze fastern yer sound. No more croozin fer her!? She's join in yer jetsets. Luvpaw*

By the time we got back to Kyro I think Valeda had had her fill of Eejippt's old-time relijun. Anuther of the wife's fondist ambishuns had allways bin to visit yer Holly Land. She hoped to vizzit Bathly Hem ware our holey thing got started, and put her feats ware the hands of Him had trod.

But frum the CNN towering noose we wotched in our hoetell it dint seem that Midleest peece wuz soon gonna brake out. Ther wuz nuthin but violins amung yer West bankers, yer Jerry Co., yer Heb Runs and yer Gazzy strippers. Alluva suddint sittin thair in frunta the teevy, we both got homesick fer gud old Parryhoot. We had bin on the go fur weaks on end, and rite now Valeda wanted to git back on her harth as soon as possumbull. She even agree to do it on the fly, wen I tole her if we book Eejip Dare to Lundun's Heeve Row we cood conneck with a jetsetter that wood git us home even before we got started!

I didden bleeve this fer a minit, I thot it wuz poppy gander wat they tole me, but the wife wuz so ankshuss fer to git back hoam she started pack-in. The plain wuz called a Conkurd witch sounds like a loozer to me, but the airheds I tocked to say it's becuz it has conkurd the distants between continence with speeds fastern yew kin make a sound.

Nex thing I noe, here we is in Heave Roe, lookin at this Big Bird that's gonna take us back to Nooyork. (But not downtown Man Hatin', thank yew.) It's a funny lookin thing, yer Conkurd, kind of like a long skinny siegel with a droopy nose like it's peckin fer dert.

I bump my hed on the way into this plain and so did the shorter wife. The ile is pritty narra too and we both had vizzyuns of clusterfoebeeya. But as soon as we got in our seets and belted up, it seem like enny uther airyplain. Witch fer Valeda ain't the best of all possibull wirls. She wuz startin to have secund thots about gittin hoam with sitch a rush, but the law of Gravol-ty took over wen her seesick pill kick in and filled her fulla groggy.

By hinkus, that plain fur shure liv up to its reppatayshin. We left the Birdish Iles at twenny minits to eleven in the mornin and we arruv at Nooyork at nine thurdeen the saim mornin! I shood hav giv the pile-it premachoor congrachoolayshins, but I wuz too bizzy with the stoowyass trundlin a snoaring Valeda off into a weelchare.

To git to yer Hamtracks train we wooda hadda go back into the senter of Nooyork. Valeda sed she'd even druther fly agin than do that. In reckrowspeck we shooda took the trane back to Trauna, becuz the wife and I wuz both overwate. They say travvle broddens, and we wuz both wider in the beems than wen we left, doo to the Calorie Stampeed we had bin on in thurteen differnt countrys. But our luggridge as well as arselfs wuz bulgin' and to git abored we hadda pay extry.

Valeda tuck anuther pill and slep all the way acrost the forty nine parlells of lassitude into Canda, so I had time to figger if all this travlin had bin wirth it. A lotta munny spent and nuthin to show fur it but sum fotygrafts, forn undyware, a cuppla tee-shirts fer Orville, and a lotta mammarys. Valeda felt the pitchers she took wuz offal edducational and yiz bean seein' sum of them fer yerself. But back home as I look over my daly diaree of the passed sex munths, them mammarys keeps cummin back to me, and it wuz jist like trippin out allover agin.

Ther wuz sum places weed of like to hav visit but we cooden cuz ther's tryball warfair goin on. Like that place that wuz Yugo Slobrya, er Slumalleya, Rue-wonder er Affagahanstand. Ther's a lotta trubble with the wirld today. The teevy noose is fulla stories about bunches of forn peeples makin trubbles fer eech uther, and watchin' all that vile-ince after supper every nite makes us deepresst and hostel. It seams we only see them forn peeples wen ther tryna kill eech other and it make us suspishus of the hole lot of them. We groops them into tribes and we treets them like we think ther all the saim.

Well sir, it wuz all this travvel that got me over that kinda thinkin. Every time I recreate all them differnt lands we bin to, I see in my mind wun or two or three individdles that we met and cant forgit. Sum of them I didden care fur, like that Roam cabdriver that diddle me outa my munny, but that don't meen I dont like enny of the rest of them Roamers. We had too gud a time ther, Valeda in the artsy galleys and me in the restrunts.

If sumbuddy is a no-gud jerk it don't foller that the rest of his tribe is too. (Jist think of sum of ar fella Canajuns.) I think if everybuddy jist jedged peeple wun at a time insted of lumpin them all in together with the rast of ther extend-it famlys, we mite git a lot more peece.

And anuther thing I fowndout—ther's morn wun way to do jist about evrything and dependin on ware ya live, anuther way jist mite wurk better ther. Us Norse Amerkens dont have all the ansers and a person don't have to be jist like us fer me to take a likin to them.

I still got a lotta curio-sitty about the resta the peeples in parts of the wirld that we hasn't seen yit . . . Honey Lulu, Honk Konk, Toke Yo, Bay Jing, Tie-one-on, Cal Cutter, Veet Napam, Camforbodeeya, Indee Amneezia, Bally, Oztrailyuah and Newzy Land. I think we'll skip Ann Tart Kicker cuz we git enuff of that kinda wether here at home. But if the wonder-lusts takes over the both of us agin, we still got haff that Blotto Sex Afore Nine munny in mewchilly agreeabull funds. And with it, sum day Valeda and me plans to circumsize the uther haff of this world.